Stoi

a..., ...e .....
Spirituality

Gentry Jones

A very thoughtful joining together of pathways important in addiction recovery. The ability of Gentry Jones to tie together what the human race has contemplated and known for centuries, along with the suggested path of one of the most inspiring movements of the 20th century, topped off by intertwining the crucially important belief gives the reader rich information and insight. The work delivers a clear understanding of the step-by-step process that can lead to recovery. This read is a valuable tool for those seeking recovery from any addiction. This well-researched work by Jones is a compelling read for all seeking recovery. A deep combination of these areas of thought is brought to life by the author's talent and his own inspiring personal experience surrounding his recovery journey. Simple and to the point.

Dale Hudler, LCSWA, NCCPSS

Dale Hudler received his Master of Social Work from Wayne State University and is a North Carolina Peer Support Specialist. Dale is the Clinical Case Manager for the Watauga LEAD Program.

ISBN: 979-8-9903019-0-0

Dedication

This book is dedicated to my family members who saved my life through their love and unwavering support. Debra, Darah, Justin, Shirley, Jason and Deborah. My recovery family is too large to name completely, but I must mention Rick B., Dale H., Susan D., Shannon S., Steve V., David P.

Acknowledgment

I want to acknowledge the members of The Promises Group of Blowing Rock, NC. The New Beginnings Group of West Jefferson, NC. And Ashe Unity Group of West Jefferson, NC, without whom I would not have found sobriety.

I gratefully acknowledge the inspiration to start writing I found by way of Miles Tager through his writing class at The Florence Thomas Art School in West Jefferson, NC, USA

A special thank you to Jed and Deb Farrington and all the Zaloo's Canoes family

Table of Contents

About the Author

Gentry Jones is a writer, poet, songwriter, and southern front-porch stoic philosopher. He's also a survivor of a thirty-year addiction to alcohol that brought him to complete ruin and eventually to recovery. In his new life, he discovered the AA 12 steps and a correlation between the steps and stoicism. The sober version of Gentry was a recent semi-finalist in the Thomas Wolfe Fiction Prize for a short story taken from The Last Turn – a novel in the works describing his life and the eventual return to sanity and serenity. This is his attempt to reach the struggling addict looking for a way out of the incomprehensible misery of addiction. His new life is filled with the joy of sobriety and the many friendships he's found on this pilgrimage.

Page Blank Intentionally

Introduction

In this world of supposedly random occurrences and inconsequential encounters, is there a common thread we can discern if we look closely enough? Is there some meaningful purpose to our existence? In the case of people like me who have lived through the misery and demoralization of addiction, when we are fortunate enough to emerge from that hell into a new world, we will notice that there are many reasons to look for another way to live. In the dark times of the newly sober or clean mind, the search for meaning and a sustainable existence is of supreme importance. We enter uncertain terrain where many lose the momentum gained through detox or rehab. We soon realize our difficult situation. Lifelong biases and fear of new ideas and concepts can make the path back into the addiction more appealing than the unknown. Fortunately for us, there are countless ways to find serenity in sobriety. This concept is the revelation that brought me to this blank page, hoping that I can find a way to put into words the absolute necessity of having an open mind to the possibility that we can move beyond addiction and have productive lives.

I found sobriety in the Alcoholics Anonymous Twelve Step Program, but I know there are other ways, and we each will eventually find our path. I have learned in my sobriety that many people come into twelve-step programs and are immediately disheartened at the mention of God and a Higher Power. I completely understand this, as it was a concern of mine as well. Luckily, I could come to terms with the belief that an ineffable force seemed to move through my life. This same concept can be found in Stoicism, referred to as logos or the inexplicable movement of life. The unseen propulsion of the universe and its actors. And so this is the concept that has led me on this journey.

The idea that allowed Bill Wilson (Co-Founder of Alcoholics Anonymous) to consider a sober life was put to him by his old drinking buddy Ebby Thatcher, who told Bill he could choose a God of his own understanding. This revolutionary idea set the ball in motion that eventually brought Wilson, an agnostic, to the acceptance that he did not have the power to defeat his alcoholic obsession. Fortunately, Bill's habit was lifted immediately after an epiphany in the hospital. Most of us have a longer, more gradual realization. It matters not how or when our obsession with alcohol or drugs is removed; for most of us, the journey to that end becomes our new life focus.

I have become fond of thinking of myself and the others on this path as pilgrims. I found that we will never arrive at a place in either time or location where we are safe from addiction, but we do have a daily reprieve, which is our responsibility to maintain. The problem is: How do we retain this daily reprieve? Is there a secular solution?

There are many ways to find serenity in a life of recovery. Through the gracious help of my sponsor and others in the program, I have discovered several ideological paths that converge at the intersection of open-mindedness and the quest for a serene, sober life. And so, at this juncture, I find myself compelled to relate to everyone searching like I was for a way to live life without a stigmatizing dogma or a meaningless, nihilistic worldview that I have found a way that works for me. It is a simple yet profound acknowledgment of the common thread that flows through Stoicism, The Twelve Steps, and *"Free-range Spirituality"* (my term for the hybrid spiritual belief in many approaches, often called panpsychism or omnism, mysticism). We can find the common thread in the ideas that focus on cultivating virtue, emotional resilience, and a rational mindset to navigate life's challenges. They teach individuals to accept what is beyond their control, embrace the present moment, and maintain inner tranquility.

We see that there is no conflict between the mystical approach to religion and the scientific approach because one is not committed by mysticism to any cut-and-dried statement about the structure of the universe. You can practice mysticism entirely in psychological terms and based on a complete agnosticism in regard to the conceptual ideas of orthodox religion and yet come to knowledge - gnosis - and the fruits of knowledge will be the fruits of the spirit; love, joy, peace, and the capacity to help other people,

Aldous Huxley, from his book - Human Situation.

One irony about the twelve steps is the fact that the word alcoholism only appears once, and that is in step one. So, the often overlooked purpose of the steps lies in the concept that we must change our approach to living to find the release from addiction. Indeed, the end of the obsession is a beautiful and refreshing thing. Still, the more significant feature of this journey through the twelve steps is the realization that there is a better way to conduct ourselves in this world. Most of us never had the tools or the insight into the mechanics of daily living to understand how far off the mark we were. Like lost sheep, we wandered farther and farther off the trail until we came to a mess of addiction, troubled relationships, and other problems we had created or decided we could tolerate.

The amazing thing that doesn't occur to most of us is that addiction is only a symptom of some more severe issues. Another fantastic thing is that we are confident most of these issues were caused by others. The union of self-pity combined with self-loathing and the seemingly infinite number of others to blame for our misery makes climbing out of this mess seem impossible.

So, here is the dilemma.

If addiction is but the progressive loss of self-control followed by a gradual slide into social and emotional dysfunction, the solution must include both a spiritual and rational approach.

I don't have a unique insight into these matters. Still, I have the experience of returning from the brink of oblivion and the many friends and family who have held me up when I couldn't stand up myself and supported me through the difficult days of early sobriety. In the rooms of twelve-step programs, we stand on the shoulders of those who had gone before us. Through the gentle guidance of sponsors and fellow pilgrims, I discovered several old philosophies and views regarding daily life that have brought me to this place. Consequently, I hope to show others looking for a way to maintain sobriety without betraying their long-held beliefs or feeling compelled to adopt religious concepts that they are not under any pressure to do either. There is a way that might not appeal to everyone on the sober pilgrimage, but I would argue that this way contains many ideas and elemental solutions to our daily challenges. It only requires a few concessions that, of our lives, are minor matters. The aggregate of these small insights can become a solid base for building a fruitful life. The basics are accepting life as it is before us, maintaining our mental well-being, and policing our bad habits to ensure we don't create new destruction. Sounds pretty simple. I wish it were so, but even the most straightforward program requires dedication and continuous growth. The daily sharpening of the skills needed to have a peaceful life and always being teachable and willing to admit mistakes as they occur are essential components of this concept.

Self-awareness and self-examination: All three frameworks, the 12 steps, stoicism and free-range spirituality, emphasize the importance of self-awareness and self-examination. They encourage individuals to reflect upon their thoughts, emotions, behaviors, and thinking patterns to understand themselves better. During our addiction, we lost sight of these things. Many of us had become so involved in the drama around addiction that we lived in a world of skewed self-awareness accompanied by seriously flawed self-examination. The inability to see and understand life in that state is perpetuated in further decline into the insanity of addiction. One goal of this book is to demonstrate that we can practice self-awareness and proper self-examination in sobriety. We need a clear mind and a positive attitude to approach both concepts in a manner that will lead to honest appraisal.

Development of consciousness: Free-range spirituality, Stoicism, and AA's 12 steps all propose a progression or evolution of consciousness. They suggest that individuals can move from lower or less evolved levels of consciousness to higher or more developed states through personal growth and self-transformation. Continued spiritual growth is at the heart of the 12 steps. This journey into a more spiritual, not necessarily religious, life can begin humbly and quietly with the initial step toward humility. Also, from the stoic point of view, the virtues needed to live a complete life include the growth and development of a conscious mind.

Acknowledgment of limitations: Stoicism and AA's 12 steps emphasize recognizing and accepting one's limitations. Stoicism encourages individuals to focus on what is within their control and accept the aspects of life that they cannot change. Similarly, AA's 12 steps emphasize admitting powerlessness over addiction and surrendering to a higher power of your personal understanding. The bad news is many limitations need to be acknowledged as we progress through sobriety. The honesty in admitting these limitations reiterates the importance of truthful self-appraisal and the knowledge that more will be revealed as we progress.

Ethical principles and virtues: Stoicism and AA's 12 steps promote ethical principles and virtues as a means of personal transformation. Stoicism emphasizes wisdom, courage, justice, and temperance, which can guide individuals toward a more virtuous and fulfilling life. AA's 12 steps also emphasize honesty, humility, courage, and accountability, which help individuals overcome addiction and improve their character. As for the spiritual side of things, ethical principles and virtues are at the core of any serious approach to finding peace and serenity in life.

Transcendence of ego: Free-range Spiritualism and Stoicism suggest the importance of transcending the ego or the self-centered perspective. They propose that by moving beyond one's desires and attachments, individuals can experience a more inclusive sense of identity and connection to others. AA's 12 steps similarly emphasize surrendering one's ego to a higher power and acknowledging the need for help and support beyond oneself.

Inner transformation: All three frameworks emphasize the need for inner transformation and personal growth. They suggest that change comes from within through self-reflection, self-discipline, and conscious efforts to cultivate positive qualities and virtues.

It's important to note that while there are these similarities, each framework has unique features and specific contexts. Free-range Spirituality encompasses many ideas, leading to a better life through conscious growth. Stoicism is a philosophy focusing on virtue and principles for leading a good life. AA's 12-step program is designed to help individuals overcome addiction while transforming their lives through continued growth.

The components of these life concepts are separately contained in countless books and organizations; there may be a way to combine the disparate pieces of this puzzle into a cohesive course of action. A common thread runs through several life modalities compatible with our search for a new life in sobriety.

And here we are at the jumping-off point, aiming at a landing zone in the field of a serene life and fruitful future. At this juncture, the decision is ours alone. Still, the caveat is once we've landed, the fellowship of the other pilgrims and the ability to grow along with our pack of kindred sojourners into our destiny is greatly enhanced, though it never will be guaranteed. As stated before, we only have a daily reprieve from addiction and are responsible for maintaining it. The problem is, how do we do that? Well, let's look into the possibilities.

An excerpt from the Alcoholics Anonymous Preamble:

A.A. is not allied with any <u>sect, denomination,</u> politics, organization or institution; does not wish to engage in any controversy, neither endorses nor opposes any causes. Our primary purpose is to stay sober and help other alcoholics to achieve sobriety.

***

"There is a principle which is a bar against all information,

which is proof against all arguments and which cannot fail to keep a man in everlasting ignorance—

that principle is contempt prior to investigation."

—*Herbert Spencer* *(AA Big Book Page 568)*

Chapter One

Step 1: Let's start at the point when we realize our lives have become unmanageable.

There must be awareness before acceptance can become our initial step into sobriety. Awareness is the understanding that a change is needed. Often, through the tired, defeated, and bleak realization that we are at the junction where death, madness, and hopelessness reside, we are offered a chance for rescue and confront the word acceptance. I often think of my arrival at this juncture as the end of an aimless journey, starting with a long, slow walk on a beautiful trail into a quiet garden filled with solitude, not unlike the feeling of new love and the warm embrace of safety guaranteed. This trek was an alluring respite from the accumulated weight of life's never-ending decisions and outcomes that were killing my spirit. I eagerly walked into this garden, only asking for some serenity and perhaps some rest from the endless race. I only needed a few hours to myself. I never intended to leave my life permanently; I only needed a break. As time progressed, there was less of my life and more of the search for peace. I liken it to the idea that a frog in a pot of water slowly brought to boiling will not be aware of the danger, instead of trying to drop a frog into boiling water. Like the frog that started in the cold pot, I had awakened in a pot of boiling water, that is my life. I am confident that had I known what awaited me, I would have chosen differently. That said, here I am in an unmanageable mess of a life. I was sick of myself, my uncontrollable obsession with alcohol, staring at the prospect of an endless cycle of misery.

At this point, I declared to myself, my wife, and my therapist that I realize my life is a miserable debacle, but it is mine, and I'm unwilling to relinquish control. The irony is I don't have the power. I had long given that up to my addiction. Somewhere inside this delusional existence arises a stubborn and hell-bent determination to never surrender. My journey through addictive insanity included detoxes, rehabs, emergency rooms, and delirious imaginings that scared me to my core, but still, I persisted in my determination to continue. In the later years of this addiction, there were moments of clarity when I could see the destruction and realize I couldn't sustain it. The saddest of the revelations that came to me was that somewhere along this journey, I decided I wanted to die by the slow, merciless killer that was once my savior. I woke up many mornings disappointed I was still alive, knowing the day ahead would be full of the same misery that had become my nightmare.

After my first introduction to Alcoholics Anonymous, I lived another eight years in limbo. I went in and out of sobriety. Sadly, few people find sobriety after their first Alcoholics Anonymous meeting. It's true, though, that some people become one-chip wonders. These lucky few never return to their addiction.

Somewhere in this murky existence, the day came when I experienced the inexplicable knowledge that I wanted to live. I finally saw a way out. I knew enough about Alcoholics Anonymous to understand that the secret to my salvation was acceptance of the hopelessness of my situation. So, I gradually climbed out of the hell that had become my life. Initially, my mind was foggy, and I leaned heavily on the people who would later become my pack.

And so it begins with the admission: *"We admitted we were powerless over alcohol - that our lives had become unmanageable."*

The first step's most problematic piece was the word "we." Long before we get to the admission of our powerless condition, the "we" must be addressed. I had been a solitary drunk and a loner by nature, and I was not looking for a social club or any other group of people to share my misery. Typical of many alcoholic addicts, I was self-absorbed, bouncing between self-loathing and self-righteous criticism of others. The idea that someday I would come to regard the folks in AA as my pack never occurred to me. As I progressed in sobriety, I realized that for me, it was the "we" that made this process work. I needed to see the day-to-day lives of other alcoholic addicts to believe sobriety was possible for me. I heard people I admire discuss their powerlessness, and through hearing about their journey to accepting the reality facing them, I could do the same. I have often thought that sobriety in solitude would be a scary proposition. I am sure some have been able to accomplish this, but for me and those I have come to know in AA, the bonds we share are of vital importance.

3

Another important discovery came when I realized I did not need to become fast friends with everyone I got to know in the meetings I attended. I found some of these characters hard to take. It took a few years for me to understand that no matter how foreign particular people seemed to me, there were genuine nuggets of wisdom in many of their shares during meetings. Once again, the predisposition to judge and separate took time to overcome. An old timer once told me that if you liked everyone you meet in the program, you haven't attended enough meetings. The growth in patiently listening to others share their stories didn't come quickly, but it has paid dividends. This idea also returns to the concept that there are many things we can't control, and the better way to deal with this is acceptance. Another old-timer quip is, "Take what you need and leave the rest."

Stoicism emphasizes the importance of rationality, self-control, and personal responsibility. This viewpoint requires honest acceptance of the realities in front of us. Step one acknowledges that the individual has lost control over their addiction and their life has become unmanageable, and that is a harsh truth to admit. This step is the simple beginning of humility and a path to a better way of life. All philosophy, including the core of religion and spirituality, are simply ways of getting to that better life.

We can apply Stoic ideas to Step One of the AA program in several ways. For example:

Acceptance: Accepting things beyond our control is one of the tenets of stoicism. The first step in the

4

Alcoholics Anonymous program urges participants to acknowledge that they have no control over alcohol. This realization is necessary.

Rationality: The value of reason in making decisions is emphasized by stoicism. Step One encourages people to see the detrimental effects alcohol has had on their lives by applying reason.

Self-control: Self-control, which is essential to the recovery from addiction, is another Stoic concept. In the first step, people must own up to their mistakes and admit that they are powerless over their addiction.

The above aligns quite well with the Serenity Prayer used in Alcoholics Anonymous meetings.

God grant me the serenity

to accept the things I cannot change;

courage to change the things I can;

and the wisdom to know the difference

The stoic perspective regarding admitting we are powerless over our addiction aligns with the 12-step view. As Epictetus said, *"Regarding things that exist, some are in our power, and some are not in our control. Those in our power are conception, choice, desire, aversion, and, in a word, those that are our own doing. Those that are not under our control are the body, property or possessions, reputation, positions of authority, and, in a word, things that are not our own doing.*

As for the body we inhabit, we did not choose the DNA that operates it or the circumstances of our birth. We did choose at some point to consume substances that altered our body and mind to the point that we found ourselves in a state of addiction. The amazing fact is that by the time we reach unmanageability, we are convinced that people other than ourselves are responsible for many of those choices. Here lies the first bit of cold, hard truth we must accept. We will never progress until we are completely honest about our condition. It may be one of the most painful things humans endure, but the truth is the only way forward. No matter how vehemently we deny our loss of control, this becomes the point where the fantasy has to stop.

"Truth is not what you want it to be; it is what it is, and you must bend to its power or live a lie."

- *Miyamoto Musashi*

That sounds a little harsh, but we have little hope for progress until we can be honest with ourselves. I have heard it said many times by recovering addicts/alcoholics, "The only step you have to get 100% correct is the first step." So, there can be no half-hearted admission or no reservations about our lives becoming unmanageable. Here is the foundation on which we can build our recovery.

At this point, we have a conjunction of stoicism and the twelve steps, but there is also a spiritual component here. Recognizing the reality of a given situation is paramount to living a spiritual life. The nexus between these three concepts is fertile ground for our base camp in which to start our pilgrimage. When I refer to spiritual matters, I am

6

talking about the ephemeral, enigmatic knowing that resides in us all but may only be realized in some. At its most basic level, this knowledge is the simplest form of the sense of right and wrong. At the core of life, the thread holds civil existence together and allows us to live sound and productive lives. It's strange how atheists, agnostics, and devout believers often find substances preferable to honestly dealing with life. The belief that life is overwhelming and without a viable remedy is far too painful to face, and this could be the turn in our lives that brought us to addiction.

So, where does this honesty lead us? It becomes the first step in a pilgrimage that will last the rest of our lives. Suppose we can accept the certainty that we are powerless over our addiction and that our lives have become unmanageable. If there is any doubt in your mind about your powerlessness, remember the many times you have sworn to yourself that you would quit alcohol or the drug of your choice only to be back in misery.

We suddenly realize that many other aspects of our lives will also need this fearless treatment. The twelve steps and the recognition that a moral code and spiritual guidance are required to proceed. Here comes the first reservation about the journey - spirituality and moral values. Now, at this place, many folks stop and reconsider their options. Perhaps there's another way or compromise available. Possibly returning to the insanity would be more agreeable.

The appropriate and often-heard phrase is that the soon-to-be doomed alcoholic addict driven by an out-of-control ego in search of peace in their life turns to the substance of their choice for their religious or spiritual needs. The stubborn and seemingly inexhaustible will to be in command of their lives propels them only further into the mire. Here also lies another contradiction that many addicts struggle with, and that is the idea that they have no ego at this point, but the truth is the ego is very much in charge. Somehow, we equate the despair we are living in with something thrust upon us by others when, in fact, our ego has brought us here and wants nothing more than to continue running the mess of a show it has created. So, we limp along in this hopeless state. Combined with a purely delusional worldview, this usually works for quite a while until it inevitably stops working. When the cold, hard reality becomes apparent that the party is over and a severe change in direction is needed, the beaten addict runs headlong into the wall, which is nothing more than the recognition of defeat. Defeat is the harshest of all things for the ego to accept, and the admission of it is even more distasteful. Here, we come to another mystery: _the confusing concept that we acquire the strength to make the necessary choices through our acceptance of powerlessness._ Another way to look at this irony is that we can choose to save ourselves through honest acceptance of our limitations. In our search for serenity, we will encounter many serious choices; the greatest is the ability to avoid the first drink, knowing we are powerless once alcohol or the drug of our choice is in our system. If there is any doubt about this, we will never be safe. While deep in our addiction, choosing not to take the first drink or drug is too hard to conceive. Through being defeated by the substance we have battled, we begin to see the options before us.

So, admitting that our lives had become unmanageable is the start of the journey into a new world. Few make this journey alone, as most pilgrims learn there is strength in numbers early on. For many alcoholic addicts, this is not an easy option as their lives have often morphed into a lonely, usually solitary nightmare. So many persistent feelings of inadequacy, separateness, and defective uniqueness make it challenging to join a group. The significance of the first of the twelve steps lies in the first word, "we." Unfortunately, most alcoholic addicts have lived for so long, alienated from their families and friends, that the idea of becoming a part of any group is not easy to grasp. We can find innumerable reasons that separate us from our fellow alcoholic addicts. Here, we find that our chance at freedom coincides with the spiritual belief that until we can see we are all connected and all we do and think ripples through our lives and the universe, we will remain stuck in the rut of oblivion.

The first step is ultimately about honesty. Even more difficult than being truthful to others is being honest with ourselves. We have operated for so long under our false presumptions about who we are and our relationships with others and the world around us that we quite possibly don't know the truth. The denial and the avoidance of the obvious problems in our lives further exacerbate the ability to surrender the egoic control of our lives. The crux of the proposition put before us to admit we are powerless over our addiction becomes only the initial stripping away of the facade we had erected. Honesty is the universal solvent. Honesty sounds so hard from this self-imposed hell in the shadows and the corners of our misery where light in the form of honest introspection has never penetrated. As many poets, saints, and sages have said, light can only penetrate through broken vessels' cracks. Perhaps thinking of the defeated addict as a broken vessel is appropriate, as no light can penetrate the darkness until sufficient damage has occurred. Another of the mysteries of addiction is where the breaking point or bottom is. In Alcoholics Anonymous, I have heard many variations on this theme. Quite often, a frustrating and heartbreaking aspect of this journey is watching others find their breaking point and realizing that no one can help them until they see it.

Stoicism is about cultivating human excellence, especially moral superiority: Courage, Temperance, Prudence, and Justice. Although Epictetus rarely mentions this directly, most Stoic texts expound virtue as the highest good and becoming a good person as the most critical part of Stoic ethical teachings. How should we train ourselves to be the best in all aspects of life?

Instead of being "obsessed with eliminating uncomfortable emotions," the Stoics were driven by the inherent aesthetic beauty of an honorable moral character.

Let's say you are an atheist, and mentioning religion or spirituality raises your hackles. Indeed, you want to live in a world where common moral values and civic responsibility create a safe and productive environment. The way this sort

10

of world works is by at least a fraction of the virtues enunciated in the twelve steps, the stoics, and spiritual values. Here is an opening into a secular life modality that can help us grow as individuals while maintaining our sobriety.

The concept that we can find our power by admitting we are powerless over certain situations may seem paradoxical, but it clears the way for us to find the courage to seek help. For the alcoholic addict, the crucial point is that they alone could not get clean or sober. This painful admission corresponds to acceptance, a cornerstone in stoicism, the 12 steps, and spirituality. Acceptance is not a pessimistic resignation but a confirmation of our willingness to find an alternative. Resistance to accepting reality is a dimension of ego that fights to maintain control of life. The ego at this point is not unlike a maniacal captain of a sinking ship oblivious to the immediate peril.

The hard truth is that we will never be able to drink or use drugs recreationally again. Here is the choice: acceptance or denial. We have been in denial for so long that reality looks like a cold slap. We can change our minds. We can reach for sanity.

So, what is acceptance?

Acceptance is a psychological and emotional concept that refers to recognizing and embracing reality as it is, without resistance, denial, or judgment. It involves acknowledging the present moment, situations, circumstances, or aspects of oneself or others without

11

attempting to change them or wishing them to be different. Acceptance can apply to various parts of life, including..........

Self-Acceptance: The ability to accept ourselves in an honest manner can be very difficult. We have to discard the layers of twisted self-reflection accumulated during not only our addiction but also the years of misinterpreting life. We have to look directly at our flaws and imperfections and realize that we are responsible for the life we have created. Hopefully, we can be satisfied with who we are, or if there is much to be changed, we at least recognize those things.

Acceptance of Others: This can be a difficult task for the addict as the farther we go into addiction, the less capable we are of acceptance of anything to do with reality, including other people. Our serenity hinges on the ability to accept that other people will have different ideas and values than we do and that we are not in control of them or their beliefs. We must accept that we don't have the power to change other people.

Acceptance of Circumstances: This involves realizing that the endless variations in life are generally out of our control and that we must find a way to process these things rationally. We most assuredly must accept the past as it is, for we cannot change it. Also, we must not be overly concerned about the future as we can have little effect on it. Our primary concern needs to be the present.

Acceptance of Change: If there is one constant in this life, it is change, and its acceptance is one of the primary steps toward a rational life. Another concept that gets lost in the madness of addiction is the ability to have an open mind, which is crucial in our quest for a more sane and rational life.

Acceptance in Spirituality: Acceptance is frequently used to mean realizing the essential character of reality and giving up control over it in spiritual and philosophical contexts. Depending on one's spiritual views, it may entail embracing the transience of existence, the interconnectedness of all beings, or the will of a higher power.

Acceptance is by no means a cowardly submission to anything that comes along. The pure heart of acceptance is the beginning of a life that more easily transcends into serenity.

Many spiritual traditions emphasize accepting reality as it is rather than resisting or denying it. Here are some spiritual ideas about accepting reality:

Mindfulness: Focusing on the present moment without resistance or judgment is known as mindfulness. Practicing mindfulness, we can learn to accept our ideas, feelings, and experiences without attempting to alter them.

Surrender: The act of surrendering involves releasing our attachment to a specific result or circumstance. Giving up control over the present moment allows us to accept whatever is occurring without resistance or fight.

Non-duality: A spiritual idea known as non-duality holds that there is no difference between who we are and the world around us. We may accept reality as it is and acknowledge that everything is interrelated and connected when we embrace non-duality.

Faith: Many spiritual traditions promote faith in a universal intelligence or higher force that directs us toward what is best for us. When we have faith, we may trust that everything that occurs is part of a greater purpose or plan.

Gratitude: Rather than concentrating on the bad things in our lives, gratitude encourages us to see the good things in them. We may accept reality as it is and appreciate the chances and rewards there for us every minute when we practice thankfulness.

All things considered, accepting reality is a crucial component of spiritual development and personal transformation. We can learn to embrace reality instead of fighting or denying it by practicing mindfulness,

"Grant me the serenity to ACCEPT the things I cannot change.

The courage to CHANGE the things I can.

And the WISDOM to know the difference."

A few thoughts on acceptance.

The stages of acceptance are as follows:

Denial, Anger, Depression, Bargaining, and finally, Acceptance

Acceptance is one of the critical tenets of stoicism.

"The curious paradox is that when I accept myself just as I am, then I can change."

- *Carl Rogers.*

A distinguishing element of the Stoics is the following: they accepted reality—the real, the here, and the now.

"Acceptance is not submission; it is the acknowledgment of the facts of a situation. Then, deciding what you're going to do about it."

- *Kathleen Casey Theisen*

The Alchemy Of Acceptance

Acceptance is the first law of the spirit. Without acceptance, we can cause ourselves immense amounts of unnecessary suffering. Acceptance is not belief, it is not

15

approval, and it is undoubtedly not resignation. Acceptance is, however, bringing peace to "what is." It's the simple act of not resisting.

- *From healtheplanet.com*

Acceptance is the willingness to let go of your emotional opposition to the reality of "what is." While acceptance sounds passive, it is not necessarily.

- *From spiritualityhealth.com*

Whatever you accept completely will bring you peace, including the acceptance that you cannot accept and that you are in resistance.

- *Eckhart Tolle*

Acceptance: In Alcoholics Anonymous circles and literature, acceptance is considered the key to understanding the teachings of the 12 steps, achieving serenity and sobriety.

From The 12-Step Glossary of terms, 12step.com:

"Recovery is an acceptance that your life is in shambles, and you have to change."

- *Jamie Lee Curtis*

Acceptance is

To be Noble,

To be Whole,

One with Heaven and Nature,

With the Enduring Tao."

- *From – Lao Tzu, Tao Te Ching,*
thehumancondition.com

"Happiness can exist only in acceptance."

- *George Orwell*

"Step One is the only step that can be taken 100 percent perfectly." - *Anonymous.*

"Step One is the foundation on which the rest of the steps are built. Without acceptance of powerlessness over alcohol, there can be no recovery." - *Bill W.*

"Admitting powerlessness is not a sign of weakness, but rather a sign of strength and courage." - *Anonymous.*

"Step One is the beginning of a journey that leads to a life beyond your wildest dreams." - *Anonymous.*

"By admitting powerlessness, we gain the strength to begin the recovery process." - *Anonymous.*

"Step One is humbling, but it is necessary for growth and transformation." - *Anonymous.*

"Through Step One, we let go of the illusion of control and embrace the freedom of surrender." - *Anonymous*.

"Step One teaches us that we are not alone and that we need the help of others to overcome our addiction." - *Anonymous*.

"Step One is the doorway to a new life, a life free from the bondage of addiction." - *Anonymous*.

"Admitting powerlessness over alcohol is the first step towards true empowerment and freedom." - *Anonymous*.

"Acceptance is the key to everything. Without it, we are trapped in a cycle of resistance and struggle." - *Eckhart Tolle*

"When we accept what is, we are free to live in the present moment and find peace within ourselves." - *Deepak Chopra*

"Acceptance is not a passive state; it is a state of being fully present and engaged with what is happening in the present moment." - *Thich Nhat Hanh*.

"The art of acceptance is the art of making someone who has just done you a small favor wish that he might have done you a greater one." - *Martin Luther King Jr.*

"Acceptance of what has happened is the first step to overcoming the consequences of any misfortune." - *William James.*

"True acceptance comes from the heart, not the mind. It is a surrendering to the present moment, without judgment or resistance." - *Mooji.*

"Acceptance is the starting point for growth and transformation. Only when we accept what is can we move towards what could be." - *Unknown.*

"When we resist what is, we create suffering. When we accept what is, we find peace." - *Marianne Williamson.*

"Acceptance is the antidote to fear. When we accept the present moment, we release our attachment to the past and the future." - *Gabrielle Bernstein.*

"Acceptance is not about giving up or resigning ourselves to a situation. It is about acknowledging the reality of what is and finding the courage to move forward." - *Brené Brown.*

So, what has this initial step brought us? I hope it has revealed to anyone standing on the edge of a failed attempt to bypass reality that there is a way forward into sobriety that doesn't require a drastic change in beliefs other than the acceptance of the truth that up to this point, we have failed to find serenity in our addiction. An honest look at ourselves, desires, and motivations is needed to create a life worth living. Sure, honesty is brutal and certainly not part of the life we lead in addiction, but it is the key to our success in sobriety.

With an open mind and an honest self-appraisal, sobriety can be achieved. There isn't any need to throw away your core philosophy, agnosticism, or other ideas about your life's purpose. Still, there is a need for honest self-appraisal followed by the commitment to correct any character defects preventing the move into a more rational, serene life.

"Accept the things to which fate binds you, and love the people with whom fate brings you together, but do so with all your heart."

- *Marcus Aurelias*

Chapter Two

Step 2: Control was an illusion.

Step two is our first encounter with the concept that we alone cannot maintain the strength to continue this new journey. If we give up our authority, what will fill the void?

Step two is merely putting the idea before us that we might not have the strength to achieve and maintain sobriety alone. We were at the mercy of our substance of choice, a power greater than us during our addiction. The irony is we certainly had a higher power during our active addiction, whether we want to believe it or not, and now we fight the idea that a different higher power can save us. We had essentially given our strength and will to the power that kept us from facing reality. In this mode, we lived in an insane world of denial. The egoic concept of controlling all aspects of our lives without the guidance and counsel of others as regards our addictive behavior eventually brought us to defeat. Who wants to admit that perhaps we need help to accomplish anything? It is strange how the idea of help from an unexplainable or even supernatural force can only make sense when we finally find the honesty to admit that our ego is defeated. Clinging to the tattered ego after being drubbed by addiction is insane, as is the idea we were in control all along.

In Step Two, we first encounter the idea of humility. Unfortunately, some humility is needed before we accept that help might be available in our quest for serenity. Hiding from life in the shadows of our addiction, we might have confused defeat for humility. The ego is convincing as regards the perception of reality. The hard truth is we aren't capable of humility when consumed with the power of addiction. So, the crux of the matter is the choice between allegiance to our addiction and finding enough humility to consider another path. There doesn't appear to be a single well-defined way out of this spot. The good news is there are many options. And so, the ego's view through its perspective rather than objective eye will begin eliminating the choices.

Like many others, I rebelled at the idea that a higher power was necessary for my life. I didn't have so much of a problem with the concept of some power or force that animates the universe, but what I was sure of was that I would not submit my life to a higher authority of someone else's choice. I fought this idea for years through my ignorance and stubborn refusal to consider the possibility that we all can have a good and varied picture of what a higher power is.

In the rooms of Alcoholics Anonymous, you will hear many stories about how people have chosen inanimate objects like door knobs or the group itself as their higher power. Most stories regarding deciding on an object usually conclude with the phrase, "until I could accept the God of my understanding." For many of us with a Judeo-Christian background, there is only one concept of God, which comes attached to some very troubling and certainly human-made baggage.

There are so many easily recounted cases of unbridled prejudice, holy wars, abuse, and hypocrisy that we recoil at signing on to that concept of God, but what is this God of our understanding? What are the possibilities? Twelve Steps programs have flourished all over the world and certainly in countries that are predominantly Muslim, Buddhist, and Hindu. One current that runs through these programs is the diversity of spiritual beliefs in any twelve-step room you enter. Somehow, in our search for a way out of the insanity, we stumble upon a new kind of spirituality, improvised to suit us as individuals. We sidestep the cookie-cutter religion we grew up with and land on a new world of spiritual and soul-enriching ideas. Could there be a purpose for us after we regain our footing? What a beautiful and unexpected turn of events brings us to twelve-step spirituality.

In our first feeble attempt to find solace from our troubles, we searched for either drink, drugs, or any substance that could give us some respite. Initially, it was not an unnatural act; we believed we had no other choice. Convinced religion was not for us, what alternatives were left? Strangely, even as our choices made our lives miserable, bowing to a higher power seemed ridiculous. Like a crazy man riding a bomb into annihilation, we continued our journey. The key word here is ours. Even as we progressed through the stages of our defeat, we became increasingly sure that religion was not for us. We persisted in thinking we would eventually find a way to make life work with our addiction.

Victor Frankl eloquently described twelve-step spirituality in his book "Man's Search For Meaning." He believes the search for meaning in our lives is the starting point of our quest for spirituality. The fact we wasted so much of life's energy on our addiction's insanity makes a higher purpose to our lives appealing. Frankl's idea is that through the connection to something larger than ourselves, our newfound serenity may be enough to get us past the doubt of a higher power.

While the stoic and the atheist look at this step skeptically, perhaps there is another way to consider what God or a higher power might be. Since physics is one of the three pillars of stoicism, physics could describe this concept as an energy that permeates the universe instead of a deity. People who describe themselves as spiritual but not religious have a conception of an infinite, invisible force that sets this universe in motion.

So, what about the philosophy of Stoicism? Can it be our stand-alone answer? Could it be an adjunct to the religious/spiritual beliefs we already have?

Massimo Pugliucci classifies Stoicism as an ecumenical philosophy adaptable to any religion or denomination – even atheism. Stoicism is a way of facing a life that presents no conflict with most known faiths. It doesn't even conflict with the idea of atheism because God is a physics-logic concept. It is not about myths or magic but reality and reasoning.

Stoicism does not require belief in a specific god or gods (logos); it does acknowledge the existence of a higher power or divine intelligence that governs the universe. Here is the nexus of free-range spirituality, stoicism, and the twelve steps.

Stoics did not have a universal concept of god or divine intelligence, and some did not mention god; consequently, there isn't a consistent reference point to logos in the many writings of Stoics. Stoics believed that the universe was fundamentally rational and benevolent and that it was up to us to align ourselves with this higher order.

The first two steps have made it clear that through the course of our addiction, we moved away from rational thought into the realm of a form of mental illness. The good news for most of us is there is a real possibility of regaining our faculties in time. The starting point becomes the recognition of our helplessness against addiction and the acceptance of help. The freeing aspect of acceptance is the first liberating step to healing.

> "Make the best use of what is in your power, and take the rest as it happens." - *Epictetus*

> "Acceptance means: For now, this is what this situation, this moment, requires me to do, and so I do it willingly." - *E.Tolle.*

"The present moment is all we have, and we should embrace it fully, without resistance or attachment to the past or future." - *Marcus Aurelius*

"Happiness can exist only in acceptance." - George Orwell.

"When we can no longer change a situation, we are challenged to change ourselves." - *Viktor Frankl.*

"The moment you accept what troubles you, the door will open." - *E. Tolle.*

"The only way to make sense of change is to plunge into it, move with it, and join the dance." - *Alan Watts.*

"Acceptance of what has happened is the first step to overcoming the consequences of any misfortune." - *William James.*

The acceptance of our inadequacy becomes the foundation we can build upon. We must find the humility to accept what is before us and move forward. Even the atheist standing in defeat and knowing that their self-will has wrecked their lives has to conclude that help is required to change. *Change* can come in many forms, so an open mind is needed. The hard work, the mind-searching, soul-searching struggle for a solution begins and will continue until we find a comfortable solution. The best part of this will be the knowledge that, at any time, our choice of higher powers can change. There was never a directive that this would be a static belief. In reality, this is something that changes many times in our lives. In the rooms of Alcoholics

Anonymous, you will hear many stories of the changing relationships between pilgrims and their concept of a higher power. Is it possible that the idea that a higher power is a never-changing deity and we must conform to its directives, or else needs to be corrected? If we are to work under the guise of Ebby's statement to Bill W. that he could choose a God of his understanding, where are the lists of this God's demands? The essence of Alcoholics Anonymous' success begins here. There are no guidelines for creating your spirituality.

You have the freedom to create the God of your understanding. What are the possibilities? Your imagination is the only limit to the options.

Indeed, in the darkest hours of your life, you have asked for strength or help. Maybe it was a plea to the sky or the universe, but it was there. Why not take the approach that you have a transient entity on your side to aid you in this pilgrimage? After all, who were you cursing or pleading with in the past? The idea of being alone on the journey you will need to take to find serenity is a daunting thought. The time for humility, acceptance, and gratitude is now. The way forward at this point may be the most expaensive stretch of the path to come. In the progression of the steps, the trail will become narrower and more defined. Now, the possibilities are endless, but the direction is constant.

Turning one's will over can be seen as a form of humility and acceptance of one's limitations. By acknowledging that we cannot control everything in our lives and that there are forces beyond our understanding, we can reduce stress and anxiety and find peace in the present moment.

Ultimately, the decision to turn one's will over is a personal one that depends on one's beliefs, values, and life experiences. Finding a perspective that works for you and helps you navigate life's challenges with grace and resilience is essential.

If you cannot conceive of a God that suits you, here are some traditional ideas.

The idea of God varies a great deal throughout cultures, religions, and philosophical schools of thought. Here are a few ways to define God:

Monotheistic God: Numerous religions, including Judaism, Christianity, and Islam, attribute the creation and rule of the cosmos to a single, all-knowing, compassionate, and all-powerful entity.

Polytheistic Gods: Various facets of human existence and the natural world are attributed to different gods and goddesses in ancient religions such as Greek, Roman, and Hinduism.

Pantheistic God: According to this perspective, the universe is divine, and God is thought to be present in everything. Eastern faiths like Buddhism and Taoism are frequently linked to this viewpoint.

Deist God: According to this viewpoint, God created the universe but stays out of human affairs and the natural world's processes.

Personal God: Certain religions, such as Christianity, hold that God and people have a personal relationship and can speak with each other through prayer.

Impersonal God: Certain Eastern religions, such as Hinduism, view God as an impersonal spirit or force that permeates the universe rather than as a living being.

Atheistic God: Instead of referring to a god with a will or awareness, some individuals use the term "God" to refer to the universe or the laws of nature. This perspective holds that God is a natural phenomenon rather than a supernatural being.

The concept of a higher power or God can be deeply personal and subjective. Here are some additional ideas about a higher power or God:

A higher power or God can be understood as a force or energy that transcends human understanding and is more significant than ourselves.

Some people conceive of God as a loving and compassionate presence that provides guidance, support, and comfort in times of need.

For others, a higher power can be seen as a unifying force that connects all living beings and is manifested in the natural world.

Some view God as an all-knowing and all-powerful being who oversees the universe and our lives.

A higher power or God can be seen as a source of inspiration, creativity, and intuition that helps us tap into our inner wisdom and potential.

For some, God is a personal deity worshiped and revered through prayer, ritual, and devotion.

A higher power can be understood as a universal consciousness or collective unconsciousness that holds the wisdom and knowledge of the ages.

For others, God is a source of unconditional love and acceptance that helps us feel connected to something greater than ourselves.

Some people conceive God as a symbolic representation of humanity's highest ideals and aspirations, such as love, compassion, and justice.

A higher power can be seen as a creative force that inspires us to live our lives with purpose, passion, and meaning.

These are just a few examples of the many variations on what God is. The nature of God is a topic of much debate and discussion among theologians, philosophers, and religious practitioners. It has often occurred to me that too many struggling people find the concept of supernatural power, an ethereal source of strength, too easy an excuse to disregard the chance for serenity offered by 12-step programs. In the ego's desperate attempt to maintain control, excuses are the escape routes to known misery and denial. Perhaps the warmth of the pan that will fry us is preferable to the cold reality we face. I contend that the step out into the unknown requires faith or at least belief in the chance something better awaits, or how else would anyone make the first attempt?

This process starts with humility. You may have confused humility with the shame you felt in your addiction; that is a common error, but humility is actually a good and necessary first step toward a sober life. This is the understanding that your deranged ego has so perverted your thinking that you can find peace in your self-imposed misery. In this regard, your ego is not your amigo!

Take a look at what humility actually is.

> "Humility is not thinking less of yourself. It's thinking of yourself less." - C.S. Lewis.

> "Humility is the foundation of all the other virtues; hence, in the soul in which this virtue does not exist, there cannot be any other virtue except in mere appearance." - Saint Augustine.

> "Humility is the true key to success. Successful people often lose their way at times. They often embrace and overindulge in the fruits of their success. Humility halts this arrogance and self-indulgence. Humble people share the credit and wealth, remaining focused and hungry to continue the journey of success." - Rick Pitino.

"Humility is not a weak or timid quality. It is a vibrant and magnetic form of self-awareness that involves a willingness to embrace all we are, including our strengths, talents, limitations, and challenges." - Robert Rabbin.

"Humility is not self-deprecation or belittling oneself; it is a quiet strength that allows us to acknowledge our limitations and weaknesses and work to overcome them." - Unknown.

"Humility is the antidote to pride, which leads to a false sense of self-importance and blinds us to our weaknesses and faults." - Unknown.

"True humility is staying teachable, regardless of how much you already know." - Unknown.

Chapter Three

Step 3: The Phoenix Syndrome

The point of the first three steps makes it clear that our malady is a three-part disease, including our physical health, mental well-being, and spiritual connection. Most of us come into the twelve-step programs with trouble in all three areas. Our situation can be traced directly to our fear-driven search for solace. The insufficient reaching for something beyond our comprehension, the long shot at happiness missed, and the cold reality of defeat. When we finally wake up and look around at the bleak world we have constructed and feel the immeasurable demoralization and panic that faces us, what are we to do? The easy way is always available and contains even more significant defeats and further distance from life and love. By gentle and ephemeral grace, some of us find the strength to choose a new direction. This new path requires surrendering our old ideas and accepting our failure as regards our previous methods in dealing with life and its trials.

While Alcoholics Anonymous is not a religious organization, it emphasizes the importance of spirituality to achieve and maintain sobriety. The higher power referred to in Step Three can be interpreted in various ways, and members can choose their conception of a higher power. Some members may view the higher power as God, while others may see it as the group's collective wisdom, the power of nature, or any other force they believe can help them overcome their addiction. The guiding principle is open-mindedness. The rooms of recovery accommodate everyone from the devoutly religious to the atheist, including a very large population of agnostics.

The emphasis on spirituality in Alcoholics Anonymous is based on the belief that addiction is a disease that affects the mind, body, and spirit. By focusing on spiritual growth and connecting with a higher power, members can address the underlying causes of their addiction and develop the strength and resilience needed to maintain sobriety.

Overall, Step Three and the emphasis on spirituality in Alcoholics Anonymous are intended to help members develop a sense of purpose and meaning in their lives, which can help them overcome the hopelessness and despair that often accompanies addiction.

So, here we are at the place we dreaded: accepting defeat and surrendering to the need to turn our wills and lives over to God's care as we understand God.

For the first time, we can unleash free-range spirituality. Those in the spiritual camp will get their chance to bat. What could be more exciting than entrusting our lives to universal energy?

As for the stoics, there are some conflicts. Self-determination and the ultimate responsibility for one's acts don't easily mix with relying on an outside power. The first chink in the armor might be the admission that we can't possibly control everything. Some aspects of our lives may require something more significant than our ability. If we permit the light to enter this crack, might we find a new way? What could be more comforting than the realization that we don't always have to be the master?

It is extraordinary how many times I surveyed the path of destruction in my wake and decided again to continue as captain. I know now that the turning of my life and will over have not saved me from problems. The problem with this process is knowing what my will is and what it isn't. This question is discussed endlessly in twelve-step rooms. The goal appears to be to find a sweet spot between the two. Patience is the virtue that brings us closer to the sweet spot. Patience had for so long been non-existent in our lives in the destruction. You will hear the phrase "practice the pause" in the rooms, as this is how patience is described. We need to move beyond the knee-jerk reactive way we were living and realize we have choices available to us if we can slow down our reaction time. Think about the many thoughtless words and deeds that were part of your addicted way of life. Perhaps there can be room for better decisions if we allow some space between stimulus and response. Just maybe this space is where an alternative will reside.

Could the patience to wait for additional inspiration be the essence of this step? It might be an answer or not, but it is a way we haven't traveled in the past. In our addiction, we were controlled by our reckless self-will. What a treacherous slope fear backs us onto. Afraid to ask for help, advice, or even an opinion, we steer ourselves ever nearer to disaster by our vainglory. On the darkest nights, we have lived through sheer obstinance and ruthless obsession for the next drink or drug, only to find ourselves depleted, defeated, and covered in shame and bitterness. There is finally a solution for us in this cold, hard reality. It requires humility to surrender our will to control every aspect of our lives to something more robust, calmer, and patient than we can be.

Here, in the early steps of an endless journey, we come across several virtues that will be important in our transformation. As we know by now, these first three steps prepare us for the serious work ahead. This bold look forward clarifies that sobriety is only a step on our chosen path. The upcoming investigation into our secrets, character defects, and long-buried fears will be painful and redemptive. On this pilgrimage, there is no safe exit along the way. We must stay on the path for the rest of our lives to succeed. The sobering fact that we will practice the third step daily is a blessing. Each new day will have unique obstacles and possibilities that require patience and the willingness to ask for help. The option to retake control of every aspect of our lives is a constant and genuine trap. The reality is that we can find ourselves in a severe state if we do. Particularly for the newly sober, the accumulation of errant decisions can create the perfect environment for relapse.

"Surrendering to what we cannot control is a form of wisdom, not defeat." - Seneca.

"Surrendering to the present moment is not a sign of

weakness, but of strength." - Epictetus.

"The wise man, therefore, always adheres to this principle of selection in these matters: he rejects pleasures to secure other greater pleasures, or else he endures pains to avoid worse pains." - Cicero.

"The moment we complete step three, we have made a decision that turns us in a new dirrection." - Anonymous.

"Step three is about deciding to live in accordance with our Higher Power's will, rather than our own." - Anonymous.

"The Third Step is the beginning of a lifetime commitment to the process of recovery." - Anonymous.

"Step three means letting go of our self-will and ego, and putting our faith in a power greater than ourselves." - Anonymous.

"In Step Three, we surrender to a power greater than ourselves, and trust that it will guide us on the path to recovery." - Anonymous.

"Step Three is the key to unlocking the door to a new way of life, free from the bondage of addiction." - Anonymous.

"By turning our will and our lives over to a Higher Power, we open ourselves up to the possibility of transformation and growth." - Anonymous.

"The Third Step is not a one-time event, but a daily practice of surrender and trust." - Anonymous.

"Step Three is about finding the courage to let go of our plans and trust in something greater than ourselves." - Anonymous.

"When we turn our lives over to a higher power, we are no longer alone in the world." - Anonymous.

"Surrendering to a higher power is the first step in finding true freedom and peace." - Anonymous.

"By turning our lives over to a higher power, we become part of something much greater than ourselves." - Anonymous.

"The more we turn our lives over to a higher power, the more we can live in the present moment and find joy in the simple things." - Anonymous.

"Turning our lives over to a higher power means letting go of the things we cannot control and focusing on the things we can." - Anonymous.

"When we turn our lives over to a higher power, we realize that there is a plan for us and that everything will work out in the end." - Anonymous.

"Turning our lives over to a higher power means having

faith that everything happens for a reason and that we are exactly where we are meant to be." - Anonymous.

"When we turn our lives over to a higher power, we become co-creators of our own destiny." - Anonymous.

"By turning our lives over to a higher power, we can tap into an infinite source of wisdom and guidance." - Anonymous.

"When we turn our lives over to a higher power, we become vessels for divine love and light." - Anonymous.

"By accepting ourselves for who we are, we open the door to a more fulfilling and meaningful life." - Seneca.

In spiritual traditions, self-acceptance is often seen as an important step toward personal growth and inner peace. Here are some spiritual concepts related to self-acceptance:

"Accepting yourself means embracing your being, without judgment or criticism." - Deepak Chopra.

"Self-acceptance is the foundation for transformation and growth." - Eckhart Tolle.

"To accept oneself is to acknowledge the whole of oneself, including the shadow side." - Carl Jung.

"Self-acceptance is the key to unlocking our divine potential." - Wayne Dyer.

"Self-acceptance is a spiritual practice that requires compassion, forgiveness, and understanding." - Pema

Chodron.

"Acceptance of oneself is the first step toward the recognition of God within." - Paramahansa Yogananda.

"Self-acceptance is not about being perfect, but about embracing all aspects of oneself, including imperfections and weaknesses." - Marianne Williamson.

"True self-acceptance comes from realizing that we are not separate from the divine, but are an expression of it." - Deepak Chopra.

"Self-acceptance is a journey of self-discovery and self-love." - Louise Hay.

"When we accept ourselves as we are, we open ourselves up to the infinite possibilities of the universe." - Wayne Dyer.

Chapter Four

Step 4: The Shadow Inventory

The Fourth Step begins the serious work required to find enduring sobriety. It becomes clear that a deep look into what has animated our lives is needed. Do we carry baggage and trauma from our past that distorts our perceptions? Have we created an egoic presence initially meant to protect us that has perverted our thoughts and sensibilities so that we have lost our original being? Who or what have we become? The fourth step's primary function is to help us discover who we are and, through the process, lead us to a place where we can begin a new life.

Step 4 in the Alcoholics Anonymous program involves taking a "searching and fearless moral inventory" of oneself. This step requires an individual to take a deep and honest look at their past and present actions, beliefs, and behaviors to identify areas where they may have caused harm to themselves or others.

Here are some thoughts on Step 4:

It is liberating: Step 4 can be challenging for many people, requiring high self-awareness and honesty, but it is crucial in the transformation from an addicted mentality to a reasonable approach to life. Although it may bring up painful memories or feelings of guilt and shame, it is a step into action.

It is an important step: Despite its difficulty, Step 4

is crucial in recovery. It allows individuals to take responsibility for their actions and prepares them to make amends where necessary.

It requires support: Having guidance from a sponsor or trusted friend during this step can be helpful. Talking through difficult memories and emotions with someone who understands can provide comfort and guidance.

It is ongoing: Step 4 is the beginning of a self-inventory process that, as found later in step 10, has to become an ongoing process. Continually reflecting on one's actions and beliefs can help maintain sobriety and promote personal growth.

Overall, Step 4 is a vital component of the AA program, as it encourages individuals to look honestly at themselves and take responsibility for their actions. Though it may be difficult, the benefits of this step are numerous and can contribute to a successful recovery.

We thought "conditions" drove us to drink, and when we tried to correct these conditions and found that we couldn't to our entire satisfaction, our drinking went out of hand, and we became alcoholics. It never occurred to us that we needed to change ourselves to meet conditions, whatever they were.

Alcoholics Anonymous 12 & 12, page 47

How would a stoic look at Step Four?

My take on what a Stoic might say about step four is you

are going to have to be painfully honest with yourself. Stoics don't accept excuses for their actions. So, be prepared to face the fact that much of your perceptions during your addiction were often skewed in the direction of blaming others. Self-reflection and accountability are prime aspects of the Stoic philosophy and can't be sidestepped in step four either.

This particular line of thought ties easily into the concept that spirituality is about the mindful and reflective life necessary to find serenity. In our quest for peace of mind vital to a happy and sober life, we can only achieve this through honest introspection. And here is the confluence of our three approaches.

Stoicism emphasizes living by following reason, accepting what is beyond one's control, and focusing on personal development and ethical living. Spirituality leads to the same need for reason and honesty. Once again, the underlying theme of the 12 Steps is the search for a new life based on reason, honesty, and humility.

While Step 4 of AA focuses on self-reflection and moral inventory specific to addiction recovery, there are some potential connections between Step 4 and Stoicism:

> **Self-reflection:** Both Step 4 and Stoicism encourage self-reflection for personal growth and improvement. Stoic practitioners regularly examine and reflect on their thoughts, actions, and values. Step 4 similarly involves thoroughly examining one's past behavior and character defects to promote self-awareness and

change.

Taking responsibility: Both approaches emphasize responsibility for actions and behaviors. In Step 4, individuals are encouraged to honestly assess their past actions and their impact on themselves and others. Stoicism also emphasizes personal responsibility, enabling individuals to take ownership of their thoughts, attitudes, and responses to external events.

Virtue and character development: Stoicism strongly emphasizes the development of virtues such as wisdom, courage, temperance, and justice. Similarly, Step 4 of AA seeks to identify character defects and correct them by cultivating positive traits and principles.

Acceptance and letting go: Stoicism teaches individuals to accept what is beyond their control and focus on their responses and attitudes. Step 4 involves accepting and acknowledging past actions, making amends where necessary, and letting go of resentments and guilt.

Step 4 is the most apparent connection between Stoicism and the AA program, but is there also a connection between this step and spirituality?

Spirituality and Step 4 of AA can intersect in the context of self-reflection, personal growth, and moral inventory. Here's how spirituality can relate to Step 4:

Higher Power or Higher Self: In AA, spirituality

often involves a belief in a higher power or a connection to a higher self. Step 4 encourages individuals to take a searching and fearless moral inventory of themselves, which can involve seeking guidance from a higher power or relying on inner wisdom to examine their past actions and behaviors. The spiritual aspect of Step 4 can provide a framework for individuals to explore their values, beliefs, and the moral implications of their actions.

Self-Reflection and Awareness: Spirituality and Step 4 emphasize self-reflection and self-awareness. Step 4 prompts individuals to honestly examine their past behavior, attitudes, and character defects. We learn that our self-reflection can be enhanced through spiritual practices such as meditation, prayer, journaling, or contemplation. These help individuals connect with their inner selves and gain insight into their motivations and behavior patterns.

Values and Moral Inventory: Spirituality often involves examining moral values and principles. Step 4 encourages individuals to take an honest inventory, looking at their actions in light of their values and ethical standards. Spirituality can provide a compass for assessing behavior and identifying areas where individuals may have fallen short or harmed others. It can also serve as a guide for setting new moral benchmarks and making amends.

Healing and Transformation: Spirituality in the context of Step 4 can offer individuals a sense of hope, forgiveness, and the possibility of personal growth and transformation. By acknowledging past mistakes and character defects, individuals can work on healing themselves and developing new ways of living that align with their spiritual beliefs and values.

It's important to note that spirituality in AA is diverse and can vary from person to person. While some individuals may incorporate specific religious beliefs or practices into their spiritual approach, others may have a broader, more inclusive understanding of spirituality. The focus is on personal exploration, connection to something greater than oneself, and finding a path to recovery that resonates with the individual's beliefs and values.

The common thread in the three approaches to improving our lives is the strongest regarding this step. Step 4 begins the work required to transition from the miserable state of our addicted life to one in which we can prosper.

One common theme you will encounter in the stories heard in the rooms of AA revolves around the concept that without surviving the ordeal of addiction and accepting the stark realization that to have any happiness and success in life, there must be another way to approach daily living. I submit to you that most of us would never have considered such a thought unless faced with a truly dire situation. Most of us are willing to admit that our life in active addiction was untenable at best and a ticket to insanity or death at worst, and we will acknowledge that a new paradigm will be needed to have a chance at a productive life.

Hopefully, through the therapeutic process of Step 4, we can understand, at least in part, the reasons inherent in our divergence from a sustainable life into the insanity that is addiction. In the searching, fearless moral inventory, we have found that step 4 is a chance at a new life. In pursuing this new life, we have just begun a process that will last a lifetime. Depending on your opinion, it may be good or bad news, but there will be many more Step 4 inventories on this pilgrimage. Conveniently found in Step 10 is a daily list that is but a quickie version of Step 4. The vital aspect of this is the daily attempt to stay updated with any issues that arise to avoid allowing them to become a more significant problem if not addressed.

We must constantly address issues instead of dismissing them and allowing them to accumulate into more significant problems. We did not use this approach before our addiction and certainly didn't use it while in the addictive state.

So, the crux of the Stoic and the Spiritual life is continuous work on our character is essential to have a happy and fruitful life, which is also the entire point of twelve-step programs.

Our first duty will be to examine ourselves.

Seneca

Chapter Five

Step 5: The power of honesty

This step is probably the most ego-deflating of the twelve. Indeed, in the rare moments of clarity, we found the ability to see our character defects in our despair, but we stuffed the thought of this truth further down into the shadows where we stored the issues we couldn't face. The truth is there isn't a human walking this planet that doesn't have an entire complement of character defects. The thing that makes it a problem for us is the fact that we didn't address them. The Stoic and the Spiritual pilgrim learn to face these issues as they arise and move on. The addictive personality ignores the character issues except when used as a reason for even more denial. Our collective hope is that through the twelve steps, we will be able to address these defects and correct them. Once again, we rely heavily on being honest with ourselves. The great lesson in the twelve steps is that we can become the person we are capable of being through honesty and diligence, not unlike the very goal of the great stoics and spiritual icons.

As it says in AAs 12 & 12, the act of admitting one's defects of character to another is an ancient rite. Religions have embraced this process for thousands of years. Any attempt to modify behavior needs a solid base, and this very act of honest disclosure is the bedrock. But remember, this is also part of the ongoing search for humility, honesty, and continuous growth.

AA's Steps 5, 6, and 7 contain the word God or a reference to a Higher Power. This isn't a problem on our journey, though. We have learned by this time we are responsible for our progress, and semantics regarding such things aren't sufficient to deter us. We can proceed with the admittance of our character defects both to another and ourselves. Always remember the ultimate goal of this endeavor is finding a better life, and the hang-up over the word God is just another of the ridiculous reasons our addictive mind finds to derail our chance at happiness.

Some claim stoicism and the Twelve-Step program of AA are very different philosophies, but there are many parallels between them. Both are blueprints and a philosophy of life; both stoicism and AA emphasize self-reflection, acceptance, and continuous work on one's faults.

In the context of Step 5, stoicism, and free-range spirituality, there are a few points of overlap:

> **Self-reflection:** A solid foundation of honest self-reflection is essential in 12-step programs. Spirituality could look at self-reflection in the ephemeral concept of the watcher and the world. In a sense, we reflect on ourselves and our past actions as neutral observers. All three interpretations eventually come to the same place.

> **Acceptance:** Stoicism, Step 5, and spirituality emphasize accepting one's mistakes and shortcomings. Stoics believe in focusing on what is within our control and taking the past as something

that cannot be changed. At the same time, Step 5 encourages individuals to admit their wrongs without judgment or defensiveness. Spirituality leads us to the same concept of acceptance: the idea that we can improve through careful, honest self-appraisal and sincere acceptance of our past.

Honesty and accountability: Step 5 emphasizes sharing one's wrongdoings with another person. This vulnerability promotes accountability and can be seen as a way to strengthen personal integrity. In Stoicism, self-examination and reflection can also involve discussing one's actions and thoughts with a trusted friend or mentor, fostering accountability and self-improvement. Spirituality is aligned with the idea that we can create a life worth living through honesty and responsibility.

Here's a partial list of character defects many of you will recognize. If you're like me, you will see them predominately in others; unfortunately, if you can see them in others, you likely have them.

Anger: Frequent or uncontrollable outbursts of rage.

Anger is one of the most destructive of the character defects. It can endanger family relationships, especially when its intensity gets out of hand. We all are capable of feeling anger; the issue is, can we control it?

Anger becomes a character defect when it harms an individual's personal and interpersonal relationships. Here

50

are some ways it impacts family and professional life.

Destructive behavior: Verbal and physical abuse can damage relationships, hurt others emotionally and physically, and cause long-lasting harm to oneself and others.

Impaired judgment: Anger distorts judgment and leads to inappropriate actions. When in the grips of anger, individuals may act irrationally and cause irreparable damage.

Interpersonal conflicts: Unrestrained outbursts of anger harm relationships with family, friends, and colleagues. Life around this atmosphere causes strain, discomfort, and fear.

Health consequences: Living in constant anger negatively impacts physical health in many ways, including increased blood pressure, heart problems, and elevated stress levels.

Anger management as a character flaw necessitates self-awareness, self-control, and a dedication to personal development. The following techniques can aid in controlling anger:

Recognize triggers: Determine the circumstances, things that happen, or ideas that make you angry. Knowing what sets off your triggers can help you prepare for and anticipate them, improving your responses' effectiveness.

Practice self-awareness. Pay close attention to the

mental and bodily cues that point to growing rage. Early recognition of these indicators will enable you to step in and stop the situation from getting worse.

Develop coping mechanisms: Seek constructive outlets and methods for handling the anger you feel. This could be working out physically, using calming methods like deep breathing or meditation, or getting help from a counselor or therapist.

Improve communication skills: Enhancing communication abilities might assist you in expressing your feelings and worries in a positive way. Potential confrontations can be diffused, and misunderstandings can be decreased by using strong communication and attentive listening.

Seek support: To assist you in controlling your anger, think about getting in touch with counselors, therapists, or support groups. They can provide customized methods and plans to meet your unique requirements.

Remember that dealing with anger as a flaw in one's character calls for work, tolerance, and a readiness to change. It takes time, but improving anger management skills and building stronger relationships are achievable with dedication and the right resources.

From AA Daily Reflections

April 16

ANGER: A "DUBIOUS LUXURY"

52

If we were to live, we had to be free of anger. The grouch and the brainstorm were not for us. They may be the dubious luxury of normal men, but for alcoholics, these things are poison.

— ALCOHOLICS ANONYMOUS, p. 66

"Dubious luxury." How often have I remembered those words? It's not just anger that's best left to nonalcoholics; I built a list including justifiable resentment, self-pity, judgmentalism, self-righteousness, false pride, and false humility. I'm always surprised to read the actual quote. So well have the principles of the program been drummed into me that I keep thinking all of these defects are listed, too. Thank God I can't afford them—or I surely would indulge in them.

"When I am disturbed, it is because I find some person, place, or situation – some fact of my life – unacceptable, and I can find no serenity until I accept that person, place, thing, or situation as being exactly the way it is supposed to be at this moment."

Anger, if not restrained, is frequently more hurtful to us than the injury that provokes it.

-- Lucius Annaeus Seneca

He who angers you conquers you.

-- Elizabeth Kenny

Speak when you are angry, and you will make the best

speech you regret.

-- Ambrose Bierce

Be not angry that you cannot make others as you wish
them to be since you cannot make yourself as you want to
be.

-- Thomas Kempis

If a small thing has the power to make you angry, does
that not indicate something about your size?

-- Sydney J. Harris

Few people have been more victimized by
resentments than we alcoholics. A temper could spoil a day,
and a well-nursed grudge could make us miserably
ineffective. Nor were we ever skillful in separating justified
from unjustified anger. As we saw it, our wrath was always
justified. Anger, the occasional luxury of more balanced
people, could indefinitely keep us on an emotional jag.
These "dry benders' often led straight to the bottle.

Nothing pays off like restraint of tongue and pen. We
must avoid quick-tempered criticism, furious power-driven
arguments, sulking, and silent scorn. These are emotional
booby traps baited with pride and vengefulness. When
tempted by the bait, we should train ourselves to step back
and think. We can neither think nor act for a good purpose
until the habit of self-restraint has become automatic.

As Bill Sees It - Coping With Anger, p. 179

Stoics view anger as an unreasonable and destructive emotion that results from our attachments and perceptions of outside events. Stoics held that external events do not cause feelings like anger but rather how we understand and respond to them. This principle can also be found in many spiritual traditions, where the focus is on our response to a problem rather than the problem itself. The key takeaway is that while anger is a normal feeling everyone experiences, our capacity to manage our reaction is what really counts. From a Stoic standpoint, rage results from irrational expectations, wishes, or attachments to things that are out of our control.

The Stoics emphasized the importance of focusing on what is within our control, namely our thoughts, attitudes, and actions.

Seneca, a prominent Stoic philosopher, described anger as a temporary madness and emphasized its harmful effects on our well-being. He argued that anger impairs reason and judgment, leading us to say and do things we may regret later. Seneca believed that anger arises from a lack of self-control and an inability to manage our desires and aversions.

The Stoics proposed various techniques to overcome anger and cultivate emotional resilience:

Acceptance of the nature of the world: Stoics urged people to embrace the fact that hardships and unpleasant experiences are an unavoidable aspect of being human and that life is full of ups and downs. Realizing this enables one to grow in serenity and become less susceptible to outside influences.

The practice of self-reflection: The stoics urged people to look inward and consider their expectations and judgments. By confronting and questioning our initial reactions to circumstances, we can better understand the underlying ideas and attachments that give rise to anger.

Cultivation of virtue: Stoicism holds that developing integrity—in particular, wisdom, justice, courage, and temperance—is the ultimate goal in life. People who practice these characteristics are better able to control their bad emotions, such as anger, and react to situations with stability and reason.

Cognitive reframing: The Stoics held that we may control our emotions through reason. One way to reframe events and reduce anger is to challenge illogical assumptions and replace them with more reasonable and realistic ones.

Patience and empathy: Stoics advocated for kindness and tolerance when interacting with people. Once again, our three methods share some common ground in this area. They thought that if we put ourselves in another person's shoes, we can better empathize with their plight and be less quick to react harshly.

To sum up, the Stoics believed that negative emotions like anger stem from our attachments and judgments of the outside world. In order to conquer anger and live a life of peace and fulfillment, they stressed the significance of developing virtue, reflecting on one's own actions, and accepting the world as it is.

Arrogance: Excessive pride and a sense of superiority.

Arrogance is an exaggerated perception of one's own importance and superiority over others. It frequently entails having a dismissive or patronizing attitude toward other people in addition to an overconfidence in one's own skills, expertise, or accomplishments. Although self-assurance and a good sense of self-worth are admirable traits, arrogance takes these qualities too far and can have a number of negative consequences. The following are important things to remember when talking about hubris as a flaw in character:

Disregard for others: People who are conceited often fail to value or give credence to the sentiments, views, and opinions of others around them. They can think their point of view is the only correct one and ignore or downplay others' arguments. As a result, one's ability to empathize, communicate effectively, and maintain healthy relationships might all suffer.

Lack of self-awareness: Inflated self-images or a lack of self-awareness are common components of arrogance. Someone who is conceited may have an inflated sense of self-worth and fail to see or accept their own limitations and shortcomings. An individual's capacity to develop and become more self-aware is impeded when they fail to recognize their own shortcomings.

Difficulty accepting criticism: It takes a lot of work to get arrogant people to admit when they're wrong or accept criticism. When confronted with criticism or recommendations for development, they might become hostile, dismissive, or defensive. A person's ability to learn and progress can be stunted if they are resistant to feedback.

Impaired relationships: Lack of humility can put a damper on productive teamwork and relationships. Dismissive and condescending attitudes and behavior exhibited by arrogant individuals can foster an antagonistic environment, escalating tensions and animosity. Trust and genuine ties can be damaged when others feel worthless or inferior.

Limitations in learning and growth: Someone who is conceited may have trouble learning from others or seeing things from other people's points of view because they think they already know everything there is to know. They miss out on chances for advancement and creativity because they aren't open to new ideas, which stunts their personal and professional development.

Professional setbacks: Arrogance in the workplace is associated with anti-collaboration sentiments, strained relationships, and subpar teamwork. It could lower morale and productivity since arrogant executives won't be able to listen to and engage their employees as effectively.

Perpetuating a false image: As a defense mechanism against their fears and feelings of inadequateness, arrogant people frequently pretend to be better than they are. Because of this, people may be less likely to reach out for help when they need it and have difficulty forming true relationships.

Being self-aware, empathetic, and humble are qualities that can help one overcome arrogance. To combat arrogance, consider the following:

Practice active listening: Get into the practice of listening to other people, taking their opinions into account, and not jumping to conclusions.

Seek feedback and learn from it: take other people's opinions into serious consideration and encourage them to be open and honest while providing input. Take criticism in a positive light and use it to better yourself.

Cultivate empathy: Try to see things from other people's perspectives, feelings, and experiences. Grow your empathy capacity through acts of kindness, compassion, and social engagement.

Foster a growth mindset: Accept the fact that you can always grow and develop as a person. Embrace a mindset that prioritizes ongoing improvement, recognizes boundaries, and actively seeks advancement opportunities.

Practice humility: Acknowledge and celebrate your achievements without minimizing the worth or impact of others. Be humble by acknowledging the value and dignity of every person and treating them with respect.

It takes introspection, honesty, and a sincere desire to change to try to reduce arrogance as a character flaw. Humble living is an ongoing process that requires consistent effort to alter one's perspective and conduct.

Dishonesty: Habitual lying or deceitfulness:

When people routinely tell lies, fabricate stories, or hide information, it is viewed as a character defect known as dishonesty. It entails willfully misrepresenting or manipulating information, typically for one's benefit or evading punishment. The effects of dishonesty on both the dishonest person and their relationships are often devastating. When talking about dishonesty as a flaw in character, here are a few important things to keep in mind:

Lack of integrity: Being dishonest shows that one lacks integrity, which is defined as being truthful, honest, and morally upright. Consistently being dishonest destroys one's credibility and brand and eats away at trust.

Betrayal of trust: Trust is key if you want your personal and professional relationships to thrive. Being dishonest erodes trust, which in turn can cause hurt, betrayal, and destroyed relationships. It makes it hard to build or keep meaningful relationships because it fosters an environment of suspicion and ambiguity.

Poor communication: Being dishonest makes it harder to communicate effectively. Dishonesty and a lack of candor in communication are the results of people who are not forthright or who deliberately lie. As a result, problems may become more difficult to resolve, and misconceptions may arise.

Self-deception and self-image: People can be dishonest if they deceive themselves about what drives them, what they believe, or how they act. Creating a false self-image, stunting personal progress, and preventing self-awareness are all outcomes of engaging in self-deception.

Ethical and moral consequences: Ethical and moral questions are brought up by dishonesty. Honesty, justice, and respect for others are principles that are violated. Being dishonest can cause a person to feel guilty, have inner conflicts, and lose touch with their ideals.

Negative impact on others: There are several ways in which dishonesty hurts other people. Damage to one's reputation, finances, or emotions might result from being duped. Someone else's well-being and decision-making could be jeopardized if they were misled or manipulated by false information.

Self-perpetuating cycle: A self-sustaining cycle is frequently created by dishonesty. It can be quite challenging for people to break the cycle of dishonesty and remain consistent once they've started. This can cause problems in relationships, a decline in credibility, and a vicious cycle of lying to cover up the first lie.

Honesty, integrity, and a dedication to self-improvement are necessary for overcoming dishonesty as a character flaw. Some approaches to dealing with dishonesty are as follows:

Cultivate self-awareness: Think about why and how often you dishonestly do what you do. Learn how lying affects you and those around you.

Practice honesty and transparency: Always do your best to be forthright in anything you do. When communicating with others, always be truthful about your goals, methods, and the details you present.

Take responsibility: Own up to your dishonesty and its repercussions. If you can, make amends and admit that you were wrong.

Build trust: Always be trustworthy, reliable, and accountable to earn other people's trust. Restoring trust requires patience and persistence.

Seek support: If you are struggling to overcome

dishonesty, seek advice from someone you trust, such as a mentor, therapist, or a support group.

Align with values: Give some thought to your principles and the significance of honesty. No matter how difficult the circumstances, always strive to act in accordance with your ideals.

Practice self-reflection and growth: Take stock of your actions, goals, and intentions—Aim to be honest and learn from your mistakes to help yourself progress.

It takes introspection, dedication, and persistent work to overcome dishonesty. Maintaining one's honor through practice

---

Selfishness: Putting one's own needs and desires above those of others:

A person is considered to have the character flaw of selfishness when they constantly put their wants, needs, and interests ahead of everyone else's without caring about how others are doing. Disregard for the emotions and needs of others, an unhealthy obsession with one's own interests, and an inability to empathize are hallmarks of selfish behavior.

Some important things to keep in mind while talking about selfishness as a character flaw are:

Lack of empathy: Having empathy—the capacity to comprehend and experience the emotions of another—is a quality that many selfish people lack. They may have difficulty empathizing with others because they fail to consider their feelings, thoughts, and wants.

Disregard for others' well-being: To be selfish is to care only about one's own happiness and well-being. Even if it means putting other people's well-being last, people will nonetheless prioritize their own wants and interests. The result might be a loss of trust, animosity, and strained relationships.

Manipulative behavior: Some people are so egotistical that they would resort to deceptive measures to get what they want or go ahead of others. For their own benefit, they might take advantage of other people's kindness, confidence, or weaknesses.

Strained relationships: When one person's demands are constantly prioritized over the needs of another, it can lead to an imbalance in the relationship and strain it. As a result, trust and communication may suffer, and feelings of abandonment and animosity may emerge.

Lack of reciprocity: People who are too focused on themselves to offer or contribute in a way that benefits others may require assistance with exchange. They may put themselves first and fail to see the value in working together, making concessions, and sharing.

Negative impact on community and society: Communities and society as a whole might feel the harmful effects of widespread selfishness. Discord, unfairness, and societal disintegration can result when people put themselves first without thinking about society as a whole or the needs of those less fortunate.

Limited personal growth and fulfillment: A lack of humility might impede one's ability to develop and achieve their goals. When people are self-absorbed, they risk missing out on chances to grow as people, form connections with others, and experience the joy that comes from making a positive difference in the lives of those around them.

In order to overcome selfishness as a character flaw, one must work on empathy, build stronger communities, and change one's viewpoint from being self-centered to being balanced and compassionate. Some ways to combat selfishness are as follows:

Cultivate empathy: Make an effort to understand other people's experiences, viewpoints, and needs by practicing empathy. Try to relate with other people by trying to see things from their perspective.

Practice gratitude: Praise and thanksgiving for other people's generosity and support can help you develop an attitude of gratitude. Acknowledge the significance of giving back and the worth of relationships.

Foster a spirit of generosity: Take part in deeds of generosity and kindness, whether they're little or large. Discover ways you can lend a hand to those in need, even if you don't think you'll get anything in return.

Build healthy relationships: Cooperation, support, and mutual understanding can flourish in relationships that are well-balanced and built on active listening, genuine interest, and responsiveness to other people's needs.

Consider the broader impact: Consider how your choices will affect people and the world beyond your short-term goals. Weigh the consequences of your decisions on those around you and the world at large.

Seek feedback and self-reflection: Ask other people for feedback on how your actions are making them feel. Find and fix your own habits of selfishness by reflecting on your own behavior.

Practice selflessness: Always look for ways to help other people and never ask for anything in return. Volunteering, donating to charitable causes, or just being there for people when they need it are all examples of what this means.

––––––––––

Impatience: Needing tolerance for delays or frustrations:

When people can't stand waiting for things to go their way or when things don't go according to plan, they have impatience as a character defect. It entails being unable to wait patiently or remain calm when faced with delays or challenges and having an intense need for quick outcomes. While impatience is normal, it can backfire if it gets the best of you. When addressing impatience as a character flaw, it is important to keep in mind the following:

Difficulty with delayed gratification: Delaying gratification or giving up short-term pleasures for more substantial gains in the long run, is a common battle for impatient people. When results take longer to materialize, they may grow impatient or violent since they focus on the here and now.

Increased stress and frustration: A persistent feeling of urgency or unease, brought on by impatience, can amplify the negative emotions of stress and irritation. Anxiety, impatience, and a diminished capacity to handle adversity are some ways this can damage their psychological and emotional health.

Impaired decision-making: People who lack patience sometimes make hasty judgments without giving enough thought to the outcomes or investigating all of their possibilities. Because the demand for quick resolution or action could impede critical thought and thorough evaluation, impulsive behavior like this might result in bad choices.

Strained relationships: Irritability, intolerance, and a general lack of empathy are all ways in which impatience can drive a wedge between people. People who are impatient often have inflated expectations of how quickly other people will respond or get irritated when others don't keep up with their expected speed; because of this, disagreements, miscommunications, and tense relationships are possible outcomes.

Missed opportunities for learning and growth: Impatience can hinder a person's ability to learn and develop. They risk losing out on learning opportunities, growth in competence, and the insight that comes from carefully overcoming obstacles if they insist on having their problems solved immediately.

Lack of presence and mindfulness: Those who struggle with impatience may benefit from guidance on how to live in the now. Their inability to enjoy and participate in the here and now can be a result of their fixation with the future or their relentless pursuit of methods to speed things up.

Impact on productivity and performance: A lack of patience can have a negative impact on efficiency and effectiveness. Since everyone is in a hurry to get things done, mistakes, oversights, and a lack of care could occur. Anxiety, depression, and a loss of concentration, imagination, and problem-solving skills are further outcomes of chronic impatience.

Impatience is a character defect that may be worked on by learning to be patient, being more thoughtful, and seeing things from a more balanced viewpoint. Some ways to deal with impatience are as follows:

Cultivate self-awareness: You need to be aware of and accept responsibility for your impatience. Consider the toll it has on your health and the quality of your relationships.

Practice mindfulness: Practice mindfulness to help you be more aware of the here and now and to train your patience. Pay attention to what's happening right now and let go of worries about how things will turn out.

Manage expectations: Be reasonable in your expectations of others and yourself. Recognize that setbacks and delays are inevitable and modify your outlook appropriately.

Develop perspective-taking: Aim to comprehend the difficulties and viewpoints of other people. Your ability to empathize and be patient with them will improve as a result of this.

Practice delayed gratification: Do something that will test your ability to wait for a reward before diving in. Doing so can help you develop a more patient outlook and increase your capacity to deal with setbacks.

Practice deep breathing and relaxation techniques: If you find yourself getting agitated easily, try some deep breathing exercises or other methods of relaxation. Reducing tension and regaining composure can be achieved through this.

———————

Jealousy: Feeling resentful or envious of others' achievements or possessions.

Jealousy is considered a character defect when individuals experience a strong feeling of envy, possessiveness, or resentment towards others due to perceived advantages, successes, or possessions they possess. Jealousy often stems from insecurity, inadequacy, or fear of losing something or someone. While jealousy is natural, excessive and unchecked jealousy can be detrimental. Here are some key points to consider when discussing jealousy as a character defect:

Destructive emotions: Jealousy often triggers negative emotions such as anger, resentment, bitterness, and sadness. These emotions can consume individuals and adversely affect their mental and emotional well-being, leading to stress, anxiety, and unhappiness.

Erosion of self-esteem: Jealousy can stem from

feelings of inadequacy or low self-worth. Individuals may compare themselves to others, resulting in diminished self-esteem and self-confidence. Constantly measuring oneself against others' achievements can perpetuate a cycle of negative self-perception.

Strained relationships: Jealousy can strain relationships, whether they are personal, professional, or social. Excessive jealousy can lead to mistrust, possessiveness, and controlling behaviors, damaging the trust and mutual respect necessary for healthy connections.

Unhealthy competition: Jealousy often fuels a sense of unhealthy competition. Individuals may obsess over outperforming or surpassing others instead of focusing on personal growth and development. This preoccupation with comparison can hinder collaboration and cooperation, affecting personal and professional relationships.

Distorted perception: Jealousy can cloud individuals' perceptions, leading to biases and distorted interpretations of others' successes or achievements. It may prevent individuals from celebrating the accomplishments of others, which can contribute to a harmful and toxic mindset.

Lack of gratitude and contentment: Jealousy often arises from a sense of entitlement or the belief that one deserves what others have. This can lead to a lack of appreciation for one's blessings and an inability to find contentment in one's circumstances, thereby hindering personal happiness.

Stagnation and missed opportunities: Excessive jealousy can hinder personal growth and development. Instead of focusing on self-improvement, individuals may become fixated on comparing themselves to others. This preoccupation can lead to missed opportunities for growth, learning, and achieving personal goals.

Addressing jealousy as a character defect requires self-reflection, cultivating self-esteem, and fostering a healthy mindset. Here are some strategies that can help address jealousy:

Self-reflection and awareness: Reflect on the root causes of your jealousy. Understand the underlying insecurities or fears that contribute to these feelings. Develop self-awareness to recognize and acknowledge jealous thoughts and emotions.

Practice gratitude: Cultivate gratitude for what you have in your own life. Focus on your blessings and achievements rather than comparing yourself to others. Celebrate your successes and practice gratitude for the positive aspects of your life.

Build self-esteem: Work on developing a healthy sense of self-esteem and self-worth. Recognize your strengths, talents, and unique qualities. Appreciate your journey and value yourself independently of others' achievements or possessions.

Focus on personal growth: Shift your focus from comparing yourself to others to personal growth and self-improvement. Set realistic goals, identify areas for development, and concentrate on your progress rather than constantly measuring yourself against others.

Practice empathy and compassion: Develop empathy and compassion towards others. Seek to understand their experiences and challenges, celebrating their successes instead of feeling threatened by them. Foster supportive and nurturing relationships based on empathy and understanding.

Challenge negative thoughts and beliefs: When jealous thoughts arise, challenge them with rational thinking. Question the accuracy of your perceptions and consider alternative explanations or perspectives.

Laziness: Being unwilling to work or make an effort.

Laziness is considered a character defect when individuals consistently demonstrate a lack of motivation, effort, or willingness to engage in productive activities or fulfill responsibilities. It involves avoiding or procrastinating tasks, neglecting commitments, and prioritizing immediate comfort or leisure over long-term goals. Here are some key points to consider when discussing laziness as a character defect:

Lack of productivity: Laziness often leads to a lack of productivity. Individuals may need help to initiate or sustain effort toward accomplishing tasks, leading to incomplete or delayed work. This can hinder personal growth, impede progress, and contribute to missed opportunities.

Decreased personal effectiveness: Laziness can diminish an individual's effectiveness in various aspects of life. It may result in subpar performance, reduced quality of work, and an inability to meet deadlines or expectations. This can negatively impact personal achievements, professional success, and overall satisfaction.

Unfulfilled potential: Laziness can prevent individuals from reaching their full potential. By consistently avoiding the effort and taking the path of least resistance, they may miss out on opportunities for growth, learning, and self-improvement. Unfulfilled potential can lead to regret, dissatisfaction, and unmet aspirations.

Strained relationships: Laziness can strain relationships, both personal and professional. When individuals consistently fail to fulfill their commitments or contribute their fair share, it can lead to frustration, disappointment, and a breakdown of trust. Others may perceive laziness as a lack of respect or a disregard for shared responsibilities.

Negative impact on health and well-being: Laziness can harm physical and mental health. Lack of physical activity, poor self-care, and an inactive lifestyle can contribute to various health issues.

Laziness may also increase stress, guilt, dissatisfaction, or unfulfillment.

Lack of discipline and self-control: Laziness often indicates a lack of discipline and self-control. It involves succumbing to immediate gratification and avoiding the effort required to achieve long-term goals. Individuals may need more discipline and self-control to establish healthy habits, maintain commitments, and persevere through challenges.

Missed opportunities for growth and success: Laziness can lead to missed opportunities for personal and professional development. By avoiding challenges or shying away from the effort, individuals may forego valuable experiences, learning opportunities, and chances to achieve their goals. This can hinder progress and limit future success.

Addressing laziness as a character defect requires self-reflection, self-discipline, and a commitment to personal growth. Here are some strategies that can help address laziness:

Self-reflection: Reflect on the reasons behind your laziness. Understand the underlying factors, such as fear, lack of motivation, or a desire for comfort. Identify the specific areas where laziness is impacting your life.

Goal setting: Set clear, realistic goals for yourself. Break them down into manageable tasks and establish a plan to achieve them. Set deadlines and hold yourself accountable for making consistent progress.

Develop a routine: Establish a structured routine incorporating productive activities and regular exercise. Create a schedule that includes time for work, self-improvement, and leisure, balancing responsibilities with rest.

Practice self-discipline: Cultivate self-discipline by setting limits and boundaries for yourself. Avoid distractions and temptations that contribute to laziness. Develop healthy habits and follow through on commitments, even when motivation is low.

Seek support and accountability: Share your goals and aspirations with trusted individuals who can support and hold you accountable. Seek mentorship or join groups that foster a culture of productivity and personal growth.

Break tasks into smaller steps: When facing daunting tasks, break them down into smaller, more manageable steps.

Manipulation: Using cunning or deceit to influence

76

or control others:

Manipulation is considered a character defect when individuals use deceptive or dishonest tactics to control or influence others for their benefit. It involves exploiting the vulnerabilities, emotions, or trust of others to achieve personal gain or to fulfill one's agenda. Manipulation disregards the autonomy, well-being, and boundaries of others, and a lack of empathy, respect, or consideration for others often drives it. Here are some key points to consider when discussing manipulation as a character defect:

Lack of empathy and respect: Manipulative individuals often lack empathy and disregard the feelings, needs, and boundaries of others. They may exploit or manipulate others without considering the impact of their actions on the well-being or dignity of others.

Deception and dishonesty: Manipulation involves using deceit and trickery to influence others. Individuals may employ tactics such as lying, withholding information, or distorting the truth to achieve their desired outcomes, often at the expense of others.

Control and power dynamics: Manipulation is often driven by a desire for control and power over others. Individuals may seek to dominate or influence others by exploiting their vulnerabilities, insecurities, or dependencies.

Exploiting trust: Manipulators often benefit from

using others' faith. They may manipulate others by leveraging their relationships, personal connections, or positions of authority to gain an advantage or to control outcomes.

Damage to relationships and trust: Manipulation can cause significant harm to relationships. The deceit, manipulation, and lack of genuine interaction erode trust and create a sense of betrayal or disillusionment. Manipulative behaviors often lead to strained or broken relationships.

Emotional and psychological impact: Being manipulated can have profound emotional and psychological effects on individuals. Manipulative tactics can undermine a person's self-esteem, erode confidence, and create confusion, anxiety, or a sense of powerlessness.

Negative impact on personal growth: Engaging in manipulation hinders personal growth and interpersonal development. Rather than fostering healthy communication, trust, and collaboration, manipulators rely on deceit and control, hindering genuine connection and personal growth.

Addressing manipulation as a character defect requires self-reflection, accountability, and a commitment to ethical behavior. Here are some strategies that can help address manipulation:

Self-awareness and reflection: Reflect on your behaviors and motivations. Acknowledge the tendency to manipulate and consider the impact of these actions on others. Develop self-awareness and recognize the underlying reasons for engaging in manipulative behaviors.

Cultivate empathy and respect: Work on developing empathy and respect for others. Consider their perspectives, emotions, and needs, and practice treating them with dignity and consideration.

Honest communication: Foster open and direct communication with others. Practice transparency and authenticity in your interactions. Avoid manipulation tactics such as lying and withholding information.

Asking for Help: It's an intentional choice to seek help in addressing one's shortcomings. This acknowledgment of needing help can be an essential aspect of the recovery journey, as it counters the tendency toward self-reliance and isolation that often accompanies addiction.

Personal Responsibility: While the step involves asking a higher power for help, it doesn't absolve individuals of personal responsibility. It's not about relinquishing control but actively participating in growth and transformation.

Respect boundaries: Respect the boundaries and autonomy of others. Avoid pressuring or coercing others into actions or decisions that are not in their best interest or against their will.

Seek feedback and accountability: Be open to receiving feedback from others regarding your behavior. Surround yourself with people who hold you accountable and provide guidance toward ethical behavior.

Develop healthy coping mechanisms: Instead of resorting to manipulation, develop healthy coping mechanisms for dealing with challenges or conflicts. Practice assertive communication, active listening, and problem-solving skills.

Seek professional help if necessary: If you struggle with engaging in manipulative behaviors or have difficulty recognizing and changing these patterns, consider seeking the guidance of a therapist or counselor who can assist you in understanding and addressing underlying issues.

Remember, addressing manipulation as a character defect requires personal responsibility, self-reflection, and a commitment to fostering healthy trust-based relationships.

———————

Greed: An excessive desire for wealth, power, or material possessions.

Greed is considered a character defect when individuals exhibit an insatiable hunger for material possessions, wealth, or energy, often at the expense of others. It involves an excessive and selfish pursuit of personal gain without regard for the well-being, needs, or rights of others. Greed is driven by a sense

80

of entitlement, an insatiable hunger for more, and a lack of contentment with what one already possesses. Here are some key points to consider when discussing greed as a character defect:

Selfishness and self-centeredness: Greedy individuals prioritize their desires and interests above the needs of others. They may be willing to exploit, manipulate, or disregard the rights of others to accumulate wealth or possessions.

Lack of contentment: Greed is often fueled by an unquenchable desire for more, regardless of how much one already has. Greedy individuals are rarely satisfied with their current possessions or achievements, constantly seeking more and believing it will bring them happiness or fulfillment.

The exploitation of others: Greed often involves exploiting others for personal gain. Greedy individuals may use vulnerable individuals, engage in unethical business practices, or prioritize profits over employees' or customers' well-being and fair treatment.

Negative impact on relationships: Greed can strain personal and professional relationships. When individuals prioritize their financial interests over the needs of others, it can erode trust, foster resentment, and create an imbalance of power in relationships.

Lack of generosity and empathy: Greedy individuals often lack generosity and kindness towards others. They may be unwilling to share their resources, time, or wealth with those in need, neglecting the opportunity to contribute positively to society or help others.

A diminished sense of morality: Greed can lead individuals to compromise their moral principles and engage in unethical behaviors. The relentless pursuit of personal gain may override considerations of fairness, honesty, or the welfare of others.

Negative impact on personal well-being: Paradoxically, greed can negatively impact an individual's well-being. Concentrating on accumulating more can lead to stress, anxiety, and dissatisfaction, as pursuing material possessions or wealth becomes the sole measure of personal worth.

Addressing greed as a character defect requires self-reflection, cultivating gratitude, and practicing generosity. Here are some strategies that can help address desire:

Self-reflection and awareness: Reflect on your desires, motivations, and behaviors related to greed. Examine the impact of greed on your life, relationships, and overall well-being.

Cultivate gratitude: Practice gratitude for what you already have. Focus on appreciating and valuing the non-material aspects of life, such as relationships, experiences, and personal growth.

Define your values: Clarify and prioritize your values beyond material possessions or wealth. Identify what truly matters to you, such as relationships, personal growth, or positively impacting others and the world.

Practice generosity: Engage in acts of charity and giving. Share your resources, time, or skills with those in need. Cultivate empathy and consider the well-being of others in your actions and decision-making.

Avoid comparisons and consumerism: Do not compare yourself to others based on their possessions or wealth. Refrain from excessive consumerism and the constant pursuit of material possessions as a source of happiness or fulfillment.

Seek balance and contentment: Strive for a balanced approach to life, finding happiness in what you have while still setting goals and pursuing personal growth. Focus on holistic well-being rather than solely material wealth.

Engage in ethical practices: Ensure that your actions align with ethical principles and consider the impact of your decisions on others. Prioritize fairness, honesty, and integrity.

Stubbornness: Being unwilling to change one's opinions or behaviors.

Stubbornness becomes a character defect when individuals persistently refuse to change their views, attitudes, or behaviors, even when presented with compelling evidence or alternative perspectives. It involves an unwavering and inflexible adherence to one's beliefs or viewpoints, often without considering new information or adjusting one's position. While a certain degree of determination and persistence can be positive traits, excessive stubbornness can hinder personal growth, strain relationships, and impede progress. Here are some key points to consider when discussing stubbornness as a character defect:

Resistance to change: Stubborn individuals resist change, even when necessary or beneficial. They may cling to outdated beliefs, habits, or approaches, even in the face of evidence that suggests a need for adaptation or improvement.

Closed-mindedness: Stubbornness often stems from a closed-minded perspective. Individuals may be unwilling to consider alternative viewpoints, dismiss new information, or reject feedback. This narrow-mindedness limits personal growth and hampers the ability to learn from others or to engage in constructive dialogue.

Lack of flexibility: Stubborn individuals need help to adapt to new situations or circumstances. Their rigid adherence to their viewpoints or ways of doing things can hinder problem-solving, collaboration, and compromise, leading to missed opportunities or ineffective outcomes.

Strained relationships: Stubbornness can strain relationships, both personal and professional. In interactions with others, stubborn individuals may appear unyielding, dismissive, or resistant to compromise. This can lead to conflicts, breakdowns in communication, and damaged relationships.

Missed growth opportunities: Excessive stubbornness can hinder personal growth and development. Individuals may miss opportunities to learn, improve, or expand their horizons by refusing to consider alternative perspectives or feedback. This can limit personal and professional growth potential.

Lack of empathy and understanding: Stubbornness often involves a lack of empathy and compassion for others' viewpoints or experiences. Individuals may be so focused on defending their position that they must listen or empathize with others, hindering effective communication and relationship-building.

Stagnation and missed solutions: Stubbornness can lead to stagnation and missed solutions. Avoid becoming stuck in unproductive patterns or overlooking innovative solutions to problems by considering alternative ideas or approaches. This can hinder progress and limit success in various areas of life.

Addressing stubbornness as a character defect requires self-awareness, openness, and a willingness to consider new perspectives. Here are some strategies that can help address inflexibility:

Self-reflection: Reflect on your patterns of

stubbornness. Consider situations where you have been resistant to change or dismissive of alternative viewpoints. Identify the underlying reasons for your stubbornness and its impact on yourself and others.

Practice active listening: Develop functional listening skills to understand others' perspectives genuinely. Make a conscious effort to suspend judgment and truly listen to what others say. Seek to understand their reasoning and consider their viewpoints.

Cultivate openness to new ideas: Foster a mindset of openness to new ideas and information. Challenge your own beliefs and be willing to reconsider your position based on new evidence or compelling arguments. Embrace intellectual curiosity and a desire to learn and grow.

Seek feedback and different perspectives: Actively seek feedback from others and invite different perspectives. Create an environment where constructive criticism is welcomed and valued. Engage in dialogue with diverse individuals to broaden your understanding and challenge your assumptions.

Practice flexibility and compromise: Develop a willingness to be flexible and open to compromise. Recognize that alternative viewpoints and approaches can enrich your understanding and lead to more effective outcomes. Be willing to adapt your own opinions or actions when necessary.

Develop problem-solving skills: Focus on developing problem-solving skills that involve creative thinking, collaboration, and considering multiple perspectives. Embrace the idea that there are often numerous valid solutions to a problem and explore different approaches.

Seek support and accountability: Engage with trusted individuals who can support and hold you accountable for addressing your stubborn tendencies. Seek guidance from mentors, coaches, or therapists who can assist in developing more open-minded attitudes and behaviors.

Controlling stubbornness as a character defect requires self-awareness, humility, and a genuine willingness to grow and evolve.

Insecurity: A lack of self-confidence or constant feelings of inadequacy

Insecurity is considered a character defect when individuals consistently lack self-confidence and are excessively preoccupied with their perceived flaws or inadequacies. It involves an internalized belief that one is inherently unworthy or inferior, which often manifests in seeking validation from others, constant comparison to others, and an overall negative self-image. Insecurity can harm various aspects of life, including relationships, personal growth, and overall well-being. Here are some key points to consider when discussing insecurity as a character defect:

Negative self-perception: Insecure individuals often have a negative self-perception, constantly focusing on their shortcomings or failures. They may harbor self-doubt, fear of rejection, or a persistent belief that they are not good enough.

Dependence on external validation: Insecurity can lead individuals to rely heavily on external validation from others. They may seek constant approval, affirmation, or reassurance to validate their self-worth, often neglecting their internal sources of validation.

Comparison and self-judgment: Insecure individuals frequently compare themselves to others, often feeling inadequate or inferior. They may engage in self-judgment, harshly criticizing themselves and magnifying their flaws while dismissing their strengths and accomplishments.

Fear of rejection and failure: Insecurity is often accompanied by a deep-seated fear of rejection and failure. Individuals may avoid taking risks or pursuing opportunities due to fear of being judged, ridiculed, or experiencing disappointment.

Strained relationships: Insecurity can push relationships as individuals may rely on others for constant reassurance, exhibit jealousy or possessiveness, or struggle with trust and vulnerability. Insecure individuals may seek validation through unhealthy means, such as manipulation or control, which can damage trust and intimacy within relationships.

Self-limiting beliefs and missed opportunities: Insecurity can create self-limiting beliefs that hinder personal growth and prevent individuals from reaching their full potential. The fear of failure or judgment may lead to avoidance of challenges or new experiences, resulting in missed opportunities for learning, growth, and fulfillment.

Emotional distress and diminished well-being: Insecurity often causes emotional distress, such as anxiety, depression, or chronic stress. The constant self-criticism and negative self-talk associated with insecurity can significantly impact an individual's overall well-being and quality of life.

Addressing insecurity as a character defect requires self-compassion, self-acceptance, and the development of a healthier self-perception. Here are some strategies that can help address insecurity:

Self-reflection and awareness: Engage in self-reflection to identify your insecurity's underlying causes and triggers. Recognize the negative self-talk and self-limiting beliefs that contribute to your insecurity.

Challenge negative thoughts: Challenge negative thoughts and replace them with more realistic and positive ones. Practice self-compassion and remind yourself of your strengths, accomplishments, and inherent worth.

Seek support: Reach out to trusted friends, family members, or professionals for support and guidance. To address underlying issues, consider working with a therapist or counselor specializing in self-esteem and self-confidence.

Practice self-care: Prioritize self-care activities that promote self-acceptance, self-compassion, and self-esteem. Engage in activities that bring you joy, nurture your well-being, and enhance your self-worth.

Set realistic goals and celebrate achievements: Set realistic goals that challenge you but are attainable. Celebrate your accomplishments, no matter how small, as they contribute to building confidence and combating feelings of insecurity.

Challenge comparison and cultivate gratitude: Avoid comparing yourself to others, as it only reinforces feelings of inadequacy. Instead, focus on your journey and develop an appreciation for your unique qualities and strengths.

Embrace personal growth opportunities: Embrace opportunities for personal growth, even if they involve stepping outside your comfort zone. Take small steps towards facing your fears and challenging your insecurities, knowing that change comes from embracing discomfort.

Dealing with insecurity as a character defect is a gradual process that requires patience and self-compassion. Embrace the journey of building self-confidence and developing a healthier self-perception

---

Perfectionism: Setting unrealistic standards and being overly critical of oneself and others

Perfectionism can be considered a character defect when individuals set excessively high standards for themselves and others, accompanied by a constant drive for flawlessness and an inability to accept perfection. It involves a relentless pursuit of flawlessness, often at the expense of one's well-being, relationships, and overall satisfaction with life. While striving for excellence can be positive, perfectionism can be detrimental and lead to self-criticism, fear of failure, and impaired performance. Here are some key points to consider when discussing perfectionism as a character defect:

Unrealistic standards: Perfectionists set unrealistic standards that are often unattainable or unsustainable. They have an all-or-nothing mindset, believing that anything less than perfection is a failure. This mindset can create constant stress and anxiety.

Fear of failure and making mistakes: Perfectionists have an intense fear of failure. They may refrain from taking risks or trying new things because they fear not meeting their high standards. This fear can limit personal growth and learning opportunities.

Self-criticism and negative self-image: Perfectionists tend to be excessively self-critical. They constantly judge themselves harshly and may have a negative self-image. They may believe their worth is contingent upon achieving perfection, leading to a constant sense of inadequacy.

Procrastination and avoidance: Perfectionists often struggle with procrastination and avoidance. The fear of not meeting their high standards can lead to a reluctance to start or complete tasks, as they fear falling short of perfection. This can result in decreased productivity and missed opportunities.

Impaired relationships: Perfectionism can strain relationships as individuals may also hold impossibly high standards for others. They may become critical and demanding, leading to strained interactions and a lack of acceptance of others' imperfections. This can hinder meaningful connections and intimacy.

Burnout and decreased well-being: The constant pressure to achieve perfection can lead to burnout and reduced well-being. Perfectionists often experience high levels of stress, anxiety, and dissatisfaction. The relentless pursuit of perfection leaves little room for self-care and enjoyment of life.

Diminished creativity and innovation: Perfectionism can hinder creativity and innovation. The fear of making mistakes or failing to meet high standards can stifle originality and experimentation. Perfectionists may focus more on conforming to existing norms or following established patterns.

Here are some strategies that can help address perfectionism:

Set realistic and achievable goals: Set goals that are challenging but attainable. Break tasks into smaller, more manageable steps to avoid feeling overwhelmed.

Embrace mistakes as learning opportunities: Shift your perspective on mistakes and failures. View them as valuable learning experiences that contribute to personal growth and development.

Practice self-compassion: Be kind and compassionate towards yourself. Treat yourself with the same understanding and acceptance you would extend to a friend. Recognize that perfection is not attainable or necessary for self-worth.

Challenge negative self-talk: Notice and challenge negative self-talk or overly critical thoughts. Replace them with positive and realistic affirmations that acknowledge your efforts and progress.

Seek support and feedback: Reach out to trusted individuals who can provide support, encouragement, and constructive feedback. Surround with people who value effort and progress over absolute perfection.

Embrace imperfection and flexibility: Embrace the beauty of imperfection and cultivate flexibility in your thinking. Allow room for spontaneity, creativity, and growth outside the boundaries of perfection.

Prioritize self-care: Take time for self-care activities that promote relaxation, stress reduction, and well-being. Engage in hobbies or activities that bring you joy and allow you to disconnect from the pressure of perfection.

Addressing perfectionism as a character defect is a journey that requires patience, self-reflection, and a willingness to embrace imperfection. Focus on progress, self-acceptance, and a healthier approach to achievement.

Impulsiveness: Acting without thinking through the consequences.

Impulsiveness becomes a character defect when individuals consistently act without forethought, consideration of consequences, or self-control. It involves a tendency to act on immediate desires, emotions, or impulses without assessing the potential risks or long-term effects. While spontaneity and living in the moment can be positive traits, excessive impulsiveness can lead to impulsive decision-making, lack of self-discipline, and adverse outcomes. Here are some key points to consider when discussing impulsiveness as a character defect:

Impulsive decision-making: Individuals tend to make decisions hastily and without careful consideration. They may act on sudden urges or desires without thoroughly evaluating the potential consequences or weighing the available options.

Lack of self-control: Impulsiveness often involves a lack of self-control or an inability to resist immediate gratification. Individuals may need help with delaying gratification, making it challenging to prioritize long-term goals over immediate impulses.

Increased risk-taking: Impulsive individuals are more prone to engage in risky behaviors or take unnecessary risks without considering the potential adverse outcomes. They may disregard warning signs or engage in impulsive actions that can have detrimental consequences.

Difficulty maintaining commitments: Impulsiveness can make maintaining or following through on long-term plans challenging. Individuals may become easily distracted, lose interest quickly, or succumb to new impulses or desires, resulting in a pattern of unfinished projects or unfulfilled responsibilities.

Strained relationships: Impulsiveness can strain relationships as individuals may act impulsively without considering the impact on others. They may make impulsive decisions that affect their loved ones or engage in impulsive behaviors that undermine trust and stability within relationships.

Financial difficulties: Impulsiveness can lead to financial difficulties as individuals may make impulsive purchases or engage in excessive spending without considering their long-term economic well-being. This can result in debt, financial instability, or difficulty meeting financial obligations.

Lack of future orientation: Impulsive individuals often struggle with planning for the future or considering long-term consequences. They may prioritize immediate satisfaction or short-term pleasure over long-term goals, which can hinder personal growth and overall life satisfaction.

Addressing impulsiveness as a character defect requires developing self-awareness, impulse control, and thoughtful decision-making skills. Here are some strategies that can help address impulsiveness:

Mindfulness and self-reflection: Practice mindfulness to develop an awareness of your impulses and automatic reactions. Engage in self-reflection to understand the underlying reasons for your impulsiveness and identify triggers that lead to impulsive behaviors.

Delayed gratification: Practice delaying gratification by consciously postponing immediate desires or impulses, learning to tolerate discomfort, and prioritizing long-term goals over immediate gratification.

Consider the consequences: Before making decisions or taking action, pause and consider the potential consequences. Assess your choices' short-term and long-term effects and weigh them against your values and goals.

Develop a support system: Seek support from trusted friends, family members, or professionals who can provide guidance and accountability. Share your goals and challenges with them and ask for their input and perspective when making important decisions.

Develop impulse control techniques: Learn and practice specific techniques for managing impulses, such as deep breathing, engaging in a distracting activity, or utilizing relaxation techniques when faced with strong urges.

Create structure and routines: Establish routines and systems in your daily life to promote consistency and self-discipline. Create plans, set goals, and establish clear boundaries to help manage impulsive behaviors.

Seek professional help if needed: If impulsiveness significantly interferes with your daily functioning or poses risks to your well-being, consider seeking professional help. A therapist or counselor can provide guidance and strategies to address impulsive tendencies.

Controlling impulsiveness as a character defect requires effort, self-discipline, and a willingness to pause and reflect before acting. By developing impulse control and thoughtful decision-making skills, you can cultivate healthier behavior patterns and enhance your overall well-being.

Insensitivity: Being unaware or indifferent to the feelings of others.

Insensitivity is considered a character defect when individuals consistently display a lack of empathy, disregard for others' feelings or needs, and an inability to respond appropriately to the emotions of those around them. It involves a general insensitivity to the experiences and emotions of others, often resulting in hurtful or dismissive behavior. Insensitivity can strain relationships, create emotional distance, and contribute to a hostile social environment. Here are some key points to consider when discussing insensitivity as a character defect:

Lack of empathy: Insensitive individuals often struggle to empathize with others, meaning they have difficulty understanding or sharing the feelings and experiences of those around them. They may be indifferent or dismissive towards others' emotions, challenging providing comfort or support.

Disregard for others' feelings: Insensitive individuals may overlook or dismiss others' feelings. They may be unaware of how their words or actions affect others and fail to take responsibility for the hurt they cause. This can lead to strained relationships and a lack of trust.

Inability to read social cues: Insensitive individuals may struggle to pick up on social cues or non-verbal signals that indicate someone's emotional state. This can result in inappropriate or insensitive responses to others' needs or vulnerabilities.

Lack of tact or diplomacy: Insensitive individuals often need more tact or diplomacy when communicating with others. They may be blunt, insensitive, or unintentionally hurtful in their choice of words or actions, causing unnecessary distress or conflict.

Difficulty in maintaining meaningful connections: Insensitivity can hinder developing and maintaining meaningful connections and relationships. Others may feel emotionally distant or disconnected from insensitive individuals due to the lack of emotional responsiveness and understanding.

Negative impact on the social environment: Insensitivity can create a hostile social environment where individuals feel invalidated, unheard, or disregarded. It can cause a lack of psychological safety and discourage open communication and emotional vulnerability.

Limited perspective-taking: Insensitive individuals may struggle to see things from others' perspectives. They may have a narrow worldview that centers on their own needs and experiences, making it challenging to understand or appreciate the experiences of others.

Addressing insensitivity as a character defect requires cultivating empathy, improving social awareness, and developing better communication skills. Here are some strategies that can help address insensitivity:

Cultivate empathy: Practice putting yourself in others' shoes and imagining their feelings and experiences. Engage in perspective-taking exercises and actively listen to others to better understand their emotions.

Improve active listening skills: Focus on listening to others when expressing their feelings or concerns. Avoid interrupting or dismissing their experiences, validate their emotions, and provide support.

Seek feedback: Ask trusted individuals about your communication style and how your words or actions may impact others. Be open to constructive criticism and use it as an opportunity for growth and self-improvement.

Practice self-reflection: Engage in self-reflection to identify patterns of insensitivity and the underlying reasons behind them. Explore any personal biases or limiting beliefs contributing to insensitivity and work on challenging and reframing them.

Learn effective communication techniques: Develop better communication skills, including learning to express yourself assertively and respectfully—practice using empathetic and validating language that acknowledges the emotions of others.

Engage in empathy-building activities: Seek out opportunities to engage in activities that promote empathy and compassion. This can include volunteering, participating in group discussions, or learning about different cultures and perspectives.

Engage in therapy or counseling: If insensitivity significantly interferes with your relationships and overall well-being, consider seeking therapy or counseling. A mental health professional can help you explore insensitivity's root causes and develop empathy and healthier social interactions.

Dealing with insensitivity as a character defect requires a willingness to be introspective and change how you relate to and interact with others. With effort and practice, it is possible to develop greater empathy and sensitivity toward the feelings and needs of others.

Procrastination: Consistently delaying or postponing tasks or responsibilities.

As a character defect, procrastination manifests itself when people habitually put off or completely disregard their duties and obligations, leading to stress, decreased productivity, and missed deadlines. It entails a pattern of doing less important things right now in favor of more pressing ones. Although putting things off till later is quite normal, persistently putting things off can have a negative impact on one's development, achievement, and health. When talking about procrastination as a flaw in character, it's important to keep in mind the following:

Delayed action and task avoidance: Even when they are aware of how important or urgent a task is, procrastinators nevertheless put it off. They may procrastinate until the last minute, which causes them to be stressed out and never get anything done.

Time mismanagement: Time management skills are often lacking for those who procrastinate. They may be unable to properly prioritize their work, may fail to account for the time needed to complete tasks, or may waste time on things that aren't related to their obligations.

Fear of failure or perfectionism: A need for perfection or a fear of failing could drive procrastination. People put things off till the last minute because they don't want to disappoint others or fail to live up to their own high expectations.

Increased stress and reduced productivity: Reduced productivity and elevated stress levels are the results of chronic procrastination. Impending due dates and the accompanying pressure to do things quickly can have a detrimental effect on both performance and general health.

Missed opportunities: People who are arrogant often minimize or ignore the ideas, views, and sentiments of others. They could reject opposing views without giving them due consideration because they think their perspective is the only one that matters. This conduct might result in relationship tension, poor communication, and a lack of empathy.

Negative self-perception: Because they consistently fall short of expectations and neglect their responsibilities, procrastinators frequently come to have a poor opinion of themselves. Feelings of remorse, inadequacy, and self-doubt may result from this.

Strained relationships: Relationships can be strained by procrastination, particularly when it results in broken promises or a lack of follow-through. People who habitually put off tasks may cause others to grow irritated or lose faith in them, which can damage personal and professional relationships.

In order to address procrastination as a flaw in character, one must become self-aware, learn efficient time management techniques, and cultivate self-motivation and discipline. The following techniques can be used to combat procrastination:

Set specific goals and deadlines: Clearly state your objectives and divide them up into doable tasks. Establish reasonable due dates for every task to foster a sense of responsibility and urgency.

Prioritize tasks: Determine which tasks are most important and time-sensitive, then order them appropriately. Prioritize finishing high-priority chores before tackling less urgent ones.

Break tasks into smaller steps: Divide complicated activities into smaller, more doable segments. They may feel more motivated to get started as a result of feeling less overwhelmed and more attainable.

Use time management techniques: To help you manage your time more successfully, experiment with different time management strategies including time-blocking, which involves setting up particular time slots for certain tasks, and the Pomodoro Technique, which involves working in focused bursts with pauses in between.

Address underlying fears and perfectionism: Analyze any perfectionistic inclinations or concerns of failure that are causing you to put things off. Ditch irrational expectations and embrace a growth mentality that views failures as chances to develop and learn.

Develop self-discipline and self-motivation: Develop self-control by establishing routines and habits that encourage output. To stay motivated, look for intrinsic motivators and rewards. For example, divide activities into fun pieces and treat yourself when you reach milestones.

Seek support and accountability: Enlist the assistance of classmates, family, or friends who can offer support and accountability. To help you stay on track, think about finding an accountability partner or joining a study group. Also, share your goals and progress with them.

Procrastination reduction is a gradual process that calls for perseverance and introspection. You may overcome the procrastination cycle and improve your productivity and general well-being by practicing practical strategies and developing self-discipline.

And so, after trudging through this list of human shortcomings and taking stock of our unique combination of these character defects, we must now be willing to do something about them. Here we take the next step.

Chapter Six

Steps 6 and 7: Hand off the baggage.

"Were entirely ready to have God remove all these defects of character."

Once again, remember as for God in the context of the 12-step programs, God is your concept of what God is.

This step involves the difficult task of preparing ourselves to move forward.

Hopefully without the character defects that have troubled our existence. Once again, our Stoics shine in this part of our recovery. The simple but effective course of action that requires humility, honesty, and a willingness to improve our character is the heart of these two steps. Also, there is space here for our Free Range Spirituality, as pursuing spiritual improvement rather than spiritual perfection is another tenet of the program. Only through rigorous honesty and willingness to accept direction can we move forward. Remember that nothing in your past or character will likely shock your sponsor. We are all amazed to discover that when our deepest, darkest secrets are shared. Once again, our terminal uniqueness is debunked.

Honesty is the key to these steps, and though it is difficult for us, we must find the courage to deal with the reality of our lives. How many of us lied to psychologists, doctors, lawyers, and anyone else we encountered during our addiction? If we move past that way of life, the only logical path is through honesty and diligent self-appraisal. So, you don't want to shine a light into that dark closet? The good news is that it usually isn't as dark as you had imagined, and many of your predispositions are common among many others. So, what is the holdup? Remember, your character defects are being laid bare to a trusted sponsor sworn to maintain your anonymity.

Key points to understand about Step 6:

Defects of Character: "Defects of character" in AA refers to undesirable characteristics or actions that support addictive patterns and impede personal development. If Steps 4 and 5 have been done with total honesty, the character flaws will already be known. Resentment, dishonesty, selfishness, fear, and other emotions can be among them.

Willingness: "Entirely ready" to be rid of these flaws. By now, perhaps, the dread of a different kind of existence has faded, and there's enough courage to face a life without the crutch of character faults we now acknowledge.

Higher Power: The term God appears right there in the text of this step. This need not distract our pilgrim who is agnostic or atheist from the work at hand. Yes, this phase calls for enough power to alter our character in the necessary ways, but where does that power originate from? That's where the concept of several ways comes in handy.

Preparation for Step 7: Recall that all we are doing here is priming ourselves for a life devoid of the flaws in character that currently characterize our existence. In the following phase, we will genuinely request their removal.

Personal Responsibility: This brings us full circle to honesty, since the rewards of this process ultimately rest only on our capacity to own up to all of our flaws.

Folks in the program often gloss over this step, but it is the first of the action steps needed to remain clean and sober. Only by admitting our defects and actively working to defeat them can we find the serenity we started this journey for. You can't shed something you do not accept. Inversely, you can't give away something you do not possess, referring to Step 12 and the concept that you will go forward and carry the message to others in need.

That sounds simple enough since we have previously admitted our character defects and are now willing to have them removed. Don't be misguided into believing that they will mysteriously disappear due to acknowledging that we have them. Indeed, the wording here may lead us to think we need only ask our Higher Power to remove these character issues when, in fact, the reality is that we are still responsible for their disposition. We may need help in this, and *sarcastically*, the good news is that this will be a lifetime pursuit. Here is a point at which a wise sponsor can help us navigate this minefield. As we discover later in Step Nine, defects will fall into three categories: ones that must be dealt with immediately, ones that can go on the back burner, and ones that may take a lifetime or perhaps even never.

The help required for this step usually comes from a sponsor's continual guidance through sobriety in daily conversations regarding character issues of concern. Once again, admitting our shortcomings is vital in repairing or destroying them. For this to work, honesty in all discussions about daily life activities must occur so the sponsor can respond with accurate assessments and direction.

On to step 7, "Humbly asked Him to remove our shortcomings." So now we face the need to have the character defects removed. Perhaps it's easier said than done, but this is actually a positive step forward.

Here are some key aspects of Step 7:

Humbling Oneself: A person can only truly acknowledge their character defects and attempt to go forward in spite of them if they are humble. The ego would be happy to deny both their presence and the necessity of continuing without them.

Asking for Help: It's difficult to change our way of life, and not everyone can do it on their own. To be sure, there's virtually little possibility of completing the 12-step program on your own—we tend to internalize our flaws. That a sponsor is involved for this reason is what makes the program so beautiful.

Higher Power: Many of us also turn to our notion of a Higher Power for support at this time in our recovery. For people who have doubts about such a being, this is the crux of the problem, but it doesn't have to be since there isn't a defined or specified Higher Power to turn to.

Personal Responsibility: We must acknowledge once more that we are ultimately in charge of our own healing, but that doesn't mean there isn't a lot of wonderful solace and assistance out there for us.

Continued Self-Reflection: This step also restates the necessity of ongoing, sincere, and modest introspection.

Preparing for Further Steps: Following this step, we still have some crucial parts of the process to work on. (Steps 8 and 9), maintaining personal growth (Steps 10 and 11), and helping others (Step 12).

And so steps 6 & 7 have been difficult for our egos and have brought to light some difficult parts of our character, and as painful as that is, we now move forward like a stoic or a spiritual being with a renewed purpose.

Chapter Seven

Steps 8 and 9: Atonement

Looking at Step 8, we find the first place in our journey that might not be completely compatible between the twelve steps and stoicism. The spiritual dimension is solidly on board with the concept of atonement. In the twelve steps, atoning for previous faults is a crucial step on the way to serenity. Stoicism comes at this matter differently in that there isn't so much attention paid to actions as to inner control and the desire to do better.

Stoicism: Stoicism emphasizes personal virtue, emotional resilience, and rationality. While it doesn't explicitly focus on atonement, it does emphasize taking responsibility for one's actions and maintaining inner tranquility in the face of challenges. Stoicism encourages individuals to reflect on their behavior, acknowledge mistakes, and learn from them. The focus is on self-improvement, growth, and living a virtuous life. A Stoic might recognize past wrongs, seek to understand why they occurred, and use those insights to positively shape their present and future actions.

Atoning for Wrongs: Making apologies or pursuing rapprochement for harm inflicted against others is atonement. It frequently entails accepting accountability, expressing regret, and acting to undo the harm done. Atonement is frequently linked to moral or religious ideologies that emphasize repairing harmony and balance following wrongdoing. There are atonement rituals, practices, and concepts in many cultures and belief systems.

Atonement is often considered a significant component within many spiritual and religious traditions, but it may not be a universal tenet of spirituality. The importance of atonement varies depending on the specific belief system and the cultural or religious context in which it is practiced.

In many religious traditions, atonement seeks forgiveness or reconciliation with a higher power or others for wrongdoing or sins. It often involves acknowledging one's mistakes, making amends, and seeking forgiveness or divine grace. Examples of atonement practices include confession and repentance in Christianity, Yom Kippur (the Day of Atonement) in Judaism, and various forms of penance in different religions.

However, not all spiritual or philosophical belief systems emphasize atonement in the same way, if at all. Some spiritual paths focus more on self-awareness, personal growth, mindfulness, or achieving inner peace and harmony without specifically emphasizing seeking forgiveness for past wrongs. For example, Eastern spiritual traditions like Buddhism often emphasize mindfulness, meditation, and the cessation of suffering without a concept of atonement for sins.

Ultimately, the role of atonement in spirituality depends on the specific beliefs and practices of a given tradition or individual. Some people find atonement a crucial aspect of their spiritual journey, while others may focus on different aspects of self-improvement, enlightenment, or inner transformation.

Making Things Right: Atonement in AA involves recognizing the harm that addiction may have caused to oneself and others. It's about acknowledging the mistakes made during active addiction and taking concrete steps to make things right. This can include apologizing to those who were hurt, making restitution where possible, and changing one's behavior.

Spirituality: AA encourages members to develop their spiritual path or connection with a higher power. Atonement often involves seeking forgiveness and guidance from this higher power to find healing and transformation.

Continued Growth: Atonement is not a one-time event in AA but an ongoing process. As individuals in recovery continue to work on their sobriety, they may encounter new situations where amends are necessary, and they strive to live with honesty and integrity.

Freedom from Guilt and Shame: Atonement within AA can help individuals overcome the guilt and shame that often accompanies addiction. Members can find emotional relief and healing by making amends and seeking forgiveness.

It's important to note that the concept of atonement in AA is not dogmatic and can be interpreted meaningfully by each individual in recovery. While spiritual principles are central to AA, the beliefs and practices related to atonement may vary among members. Ultimately, the goal is to achieve and maintain sobriety while fostering personal growth and positive relationships with others.

Atonement and spirituality are interconnected concepts that often appear in religious, moral, and philosophical contexts. Both involve seeking reconciliation, restoration, and healing, but they manifest differently and hold distinct meanings in various belief systems.

Atonement refers to making amends or seeking reconciliation for wrongdoing or harm caused to oneself, others, or a higher power. It involves acknowledging responsibility, expressing remorse, and taking action to rectify the damage caused. Atonement is often associated with restoring balance, harmony, and moral order. Different cultures, religions, and ethical frameworks have interpretations and practices related to atonement.

Spirituality: A person's connection to anything beyond the material world is referred to as spirituality, which is a more general term that frequently includes the pursuit of meaning, purpose, and a deeper comprehension of existence. Spirituality isn't just about religion; it may also be about feeling awed, amazed, and connected to the universe, nature, or a greater force. Spiritual activities frequently involve prayer, meditation, introspection, and the pursuit of enlightenment and personal development.

The relationship between spirituality and atonement:

Healing and Growth: Spirituality and atonement provide avenues for healing and human development. By addressing past wrongs and asking for forgiveness, atonement enables people to move toward emotional health and development. A foundation for introspection and self-realization is offered by spirituality, which enhances well-being.

Seeking Connection: Seeking connection and reconciliation with others is a common aspect of atonement, with a focus on mending relationships. People who identify as spiritual look for a way to connect with a transcendent reality, which could be the universe, a higher power, or a group consciousness.

Transcendence and Redemption: Themes of transcendence and salvation may be included in both conceptions. A sense of transcendence beyond the ordinary parts of life is commonly sought after in spirituality, whereas atonement aims to atone for one's deeds and restore moral equilibrium.

Rituals and Practices: Atonement-related rites and customs, such as acts of reparation, confession, and repentance, are a part of many religious traditions. In

115

a similar vein, spiritual disciplines like mindfulness and meditation can help people become more self-aware and have a better knowledge of their behaviors and their effects.

Ethical Living: Spirituality and atonement frequently encourage moral life. In line with moral principles, atonement motivates people to accept accountability for their deeds and make restitution. Living in accordance with one's spiritual beliefs promotes integrity and a sense of purpose in life.

Cultural Variations: Different cultures and religions have different ways of seeking forgiveness and reconciliation, which is reflected in their varied approaches to atonement practices. Cultural influences also have an impact on spirituality, resulting in a variety of rituals and beliefs that direct people in their search for purpose and connection.

In conclusion, the ideas of healing, development, connection, and redemption are shared by both spirituality and atonement. While spirituality includes a broader desire for connection to anything beyond the material world, atonement is primarily focused on confronting past wrongs and seeking reconciliation; this search frequently results in personal transformation and a feeling of purpose. The interaction of these ideas reveals the richness and complexity of human desires and experiences.

Chapter Eight

Step 10: The daily maintenance

Alcoholics Anonymous 10th Step and Stoicism share similarities in their principles and goals but also have distinct differences. Let's compare the two:

Alcoholics Anonymous

Continued to take personal inventory and, when we were wrong, promptly admitted it.

The important thing here is we are preparing for a new life, a new way to live amid the daily struggles and joys that we could not handle in our previous life. The importance of honesty about our life situation is the point of this step. We have learned the cost of our inability to admit the truth about our reactions to the world's often painful occurrences. The truly mysterious thing is the good times could often be as difficult as the tragedies for us to reconcile. So, we come to this point in our recovery where we must courageously look at each day's actions and thoughts honestly and look for ways to improve.

Self-examination: Making a daily inventory of one's thoughts, deeds, and behaviors is part of the AA 10th step. It invites people to take stock of their day and pinpoint any grudges, anxieties, or other unfavorable feelings that could have surfaced.

Amends: It also stresses quickly making amends

when one is wrong, encouraging responsibility and development on a personal level.

Continual Self-Improvement: By addressing problems as they come up and preventing relapse, this step aims to sustain sobriety and encourage ongoing self-improvement. The goal of this phase, like with the stoics, is to increase self-awareness by thorough introspection.

Stoicism:

Self-examination: Self-examination is encouraged by stoicism, although it does so within a larger philosophical framework. Stoics hold that virtue and peace can only be attained by being self-aware and comprehending one's feelings and judgments.

Acceptance and Control: The duality of control is emphasized by stoicism, which encourages people to accept what they cannot control (outside occurrences and other people's actions) and concentrate on what they can control, such as their attitudes and behaviors. This strikes at the core of everyday self-evaluation because the majority of our challenges are related to realizing what is within our control and what is not and how our perspective of these things impacts our existence.

Virtue and Eudaimonia: Pursuing virtue and eudaimonia—the belief that happiness and personal well-being are the ultimate ethical goals—are the main focal points of stoicism. It teaches that a happy and meaningful life can be had by living in harmony with nature and displaying courage, justice, wisdom, and temperance.

Comparison:

Self-Examination: AA's 10th step and Stoicism stress the importance of self-examination. However, AA focuses on addressing specific issues related to addiction recovery, while Stoicism's self-examination has a broader philosophical aim of achieving wisdom and tranquility. Don't assume that the AA approach to Step Ten is geared mainly at maintaining sobriety; all the steps aim to create a new approach to life in the future.

Responsibility and Accountability: AA strongly emphasizes taking responsibility for one's actions and making amends, a crucial aspect of addiction recovery. Stoicism also promotes personal responsibility within a broader context of accepting external events.

End Goals: The end goals of Stoicism and Alcoholics Anonymous differ only as much as one is a philosophy that may be embarked on at any time during a person's life, whereas Alcoholics Anonymous and especially the tenth step is encountered after a person has realized they need a new way to organize their life. Unfortunately, the alcoholic has come to need this through a traumatic and demoralizing course of events. It does not diminish that person's honest desire for a new way of life; the need to change may stiffen their resolve to adhere to this new philosophical approach. Like the stoic adherent, the goal is to attain virtue, inner peace, and eudaimonia, which can apply to anyone, whether they have struggled with addiction.

A fitting quote from Quintus Sextius regarding taking a daily inventory of oneself.

> What ailment of yours have you cured today? What failings have you resisted? Where can you show improvement?

The beauty of this step is that it embodies many aspects of stoicism, spirituality, and the idea of perpetual improvement, which is paramount in the 12 steps. This concept is heard in many 12-step meetings in the phrase that we seek spiritual growth, not perfection.

"Your world is a living expression of how you are using and have used your mind."

Earl Nightingale

You will hear in twelve-step meetings that the purpose of Alcoholics Anonymous is to develop a better way to live. We found our way to Alcoholics Anonymous because we did not have the tools to deal with life as we found it. Life would have been much different if we had enough understanding of our insecurities, character defects, and responsibility for our life's view. Like the quote from Earl

Nightingale, we were living in a dysfunctional world that we either created or, through convoluted thinking, resigned ourselves to tolerate. The great triumph of the journey through sobriety must involve personal growth, or we risk becoming a dry drunk. This term refers to a sad state in which a person is sober and miserable. Being sober and not growing in the ability to navigate life is a prescription for sorrow, heartbreak, and, most likely, another drunk. The steps point us toward finding the tools to participate in life in a way we didn't know. I contend stoicism and spirituality do the same. I believe a combination of all three and the willingness to have an open mind makes this journey essential in the search for serenity.

Daily self-appraisal, self-reflection, or self-assessment can be valuable for personal growth and development. Here are some thoughts on daily self-appraisal:

Increased Self-Awareness: Regularly assessing your thoughts, actions, and feelings can help you better understand yourself. Self-awareness is crucial for personal growth because it allows you to identify your strengths and weaknesses.

Goal Setting: Self-appraisal can help you set and track your goals effectively. By evaluating your progress daily, you can make necessary adjustments to stay on course and achieve your objectives.

Improved Decision-Making: Reflecting on your daily choices and actions can help you make better decisions in the future. It allows you to learn from your mistakes and build on your successes.

Accountability: Self-appraisal holds you accountable for your actions. Regularly evaluating your behavior makes you more responsible for your choices and consequences.

Stress Reduction: Self-reflection can also help reduce stress and anxiety. By processing your thoughts and emotions, you can address any issues or concerns that may be causing stress and work towards solutions.

Increased Empathy: Daily self-appraisal can enhance your empathy towards others. As you become more in tune with your emotions and experiences, you may understand others' perspectives and feelings.

Continuous Learning: Life is a constant learning process, and self-appraisal helps facilitate this journey. It encourages you to seek new knowledge and experiences and to adapt to changing circumstances.

Building Resilience: You can develop resilience by examining your daily challenges and setbacks. Bouncing back from failures and setbacks is essential for personal and professional growth.

Positive Reinforcement: Celebrating your daily achievements, no matter how small, can boost your self-esteem and motivation. Recognizing your progress can be a powerful incentive to keep moving forward.

Healthy Relationships: Self-reflection can also benefit your relationships. When you understand yourself better, you can communicate your needs and boundaries more effectively, leading to healthier interactions with others.

However, it's important to approach daily self-appraisal with balance. Overanalyzing or being overly critical of yourself can be counterproductive and lead to self-doubt. It's essential to maintain a positive and constructive mindset during this process. Daily self-appraisal may not suit everyone, and some may find weekly or monthly reflections more manageable and effective.

Consistency and commitment to personal growth are the key to successful daily self-appraisal. It's a practice that can help you navigate life's challenges and become the best version of yourself

Self-examination is a deliberate process of introspection and reflection on one's thoughts, feelings, behaviors, and life experiences. It involves critically examining oneself, one's values, beliefs, and actions to gain insight, improve, and grow.

The Intersection of Spirituality and Self-Examination: Spirituality and self-examination intersect in several ways:

Self-Awareness: Spirituality encourages self-awareness by prompting individuals to explore their inner world, values, and beliefs. Self-examination is a key component of this process, as it helps individuals understand their motivations and actions in the context of their spiritual journey.

Values and Morality: Spirituality often involves the development of a moral or ethical framework. Self-examination allows individuals to assess whether their actions align with their spiritual values and principles. It can help identify areas where personal growth or moral development is needed.

Seeking Meaning and Purpose: Many people turn to spirituality to find meaning and purpose. Self-examination can be a tool for individuals to clarify their personal values and life goals, thereby contributing to their sense of purpose.

Inner Peace and Fulfillment: Spirituality often seeks inner peace and fulfillment. Self-examination can help identify inner conflicts, unresolved issues, or emotional baggage that may hinder one's spiritual journey. Individuals can achieve greater peace and fulfillment by addressing these issues through self-reflection.

Lifelong Growth: Both spirituality and self-examination promote ongoing personal growth and development. As individuals engage in self-examination, they may discover new aspects of their spirituality and adjust their beliefs or practices over time.

Practices for Spiritual Self-Examination:

Journaling: Keeping a spiritual journal to record thoughts, experiences, and reflections.

Meditation and Mindfulness: These practices can facilitate self-examination by promoting present-moment awareness.

Retreats and Solitude: Taking time away from daily life to reflect and reconnect with one's spirituality.

Conversations and Guidance: Engaging in meaningful discussions with mentors, counselors, or fellow seekers.

Chapter Nine

Step 11: Spiritual Connectivity

"Sought through prayer and meditation to improve our conscious contact with God as we understood Him praying only for knowledge of his will for us and the power to carry that out."

Here we come to the mention of God, and thankfully not just God but the God of our understanding. And so, what does that mean exactly? It has meant and continues to mean many different things to many people. I have taken it to mean the ineffable force that animates this universe. This definition works for me, but many others have found similar and varied explanations for the term. The bottom line is that it can mean whatever you need it to mean as long as you are willing to admit that you are not God and that your life has been a mess under your direction. For all the alcoholics I have known, the part of their story that is common to all is the realization that they had ruined their own lives by themselves and will run riot. The tragic confusion between self-loathing and righteous self-centeredness and the conviction that the world and its inhabitants have conspired to destroy our serenity justifies any means of escape from reality.

I believe the insertion of God into the 12 steps came in part because the founders were searching for a power greater than themselves to rely on once they realized their inability to manage their lives had more to do with their obsessions than alcohol or the drug they chose. Their obsessions were only a symptom of the desperate cry for help. This cry for help is in a misguided direction.

And so, what are we to do if we still have an issue with God? Do you have the courage and the strength to move forward independently? I have heard many alcoholics refer to GOD as an acronym for "Group Of Drunks" or "Good Orderly Direction." The possibilities are infinite.

A common phrase heard in the rooms of 12-step meetings is "stay in the pack." In other terms, "keep coming back." For many, this becomes their interpretation of God. Perhaps the knowledge that there are others in the same boat and together, there is a greater chance of survival.

This step continues to be difficult to reconcile with stoicism, as we are asked to improve our conscious contact with God through prayer and meditation. Indeed, if we don't have a well-defined idea of God, how can we pray to increase our conscious contact with this entity? A stoic would approach this as another opportunity to reflect on our limitations and better understand how to move forward.

To a stoic, what is God's will? I believe this would be the natural flow of life, the constant evolution of the daily process we go through. The stoic understands and accepts that this ever-unfolding play that we are an actor in is the essence of life. An essential part of stoicism is Amor Fati, or the love of fate. This aligns with the often-heard phrase, "It is as it should be." Much like the Tao.

Is this what humans, for centuries, have understood to be God?

So, how do you create and maintain a better relationship with this process? The answer may be as simple as the instruction found in step 11 to improve our conscious contact with this evolving play that our part is woven into. Not to dismiss anyone's concept of God as a definable entity, but only to make the argument that perhaps the force that moves this universal stage production forward is the essence of God as a stoic might see it. And so if this is, in fact, a viable means for the agnostic or atheist to find peace in the 12-step process, all the better. The final goal of Alcoholics Anonymous is the need to share our experiences with others in an effort to help them find a way into sobriety. Always, we must remember that sobriety is only the beginning of a better life that is revealed to us as we work the 12 steps. The beauty of the 12 steps, in fact, is a blueprint for life, not very different from any philosophical or spiritual/religious doctrine. The biggest difference is the freedom that the 12 steps allow so the individual can interpret the suggestions themselves.

So, regarding how a Stoic might think of God's will, it's important to consider that Stoicism doesn't conceptualize God in the same way as some religious traditions. Instead, a Stoic might approach the idea of God's will in the following ways:

Harmony with Nature: Living in harmony with nature meant acknowledging the natural order of the

128

universe, according to stoic philosophy. If one were to understand God's will in terms of the Stoics, it would be equivalent with this natural and rational order since they would see circumstances and events as a part of this cosmic order.

Acceptance of Fate: (Love of Fate, Amor Fati) Accepting what we cannot alter and concentrating on what we can influence are lessons stoicism imparts. A stoic would view God's will as the immutable parts of reality, and it would be prudent to accept these parts and modify one's actions and mindset accordingly.

Moral Virtue:(Maximum Bonum: The Ultimate Good) Living a virtuous life and moral character are highly valued in stoicism. Given that the Logos is frequently connected to virtue and reason, a Stoic may understand God's will as an exhortation to live morally upright lives.

Inner Peace: Stoicism places a strong emphasis on using reason and self-control to achieve inner calm and tranquility. Following God's will, according to a Stoic perspective, would entail finding inner tranquility by coordinating one's thoughts and deeds with virtue and reason.

To sum up, although stoicism lacks the traditional conception of God that many religious traditions possess, a stoic understanding of God's will would probably center on living in balance with the natural world, acknowledging the order of things as they are, and pursuing moral excellence and inner tranquility. Rather than religious or theological issues, this perspective is more aligned with ethical and rational ones.

In this step, our free-range spiritualism is quite at home, as meditation and prayer are essential to increased contact with our spiritual essence.

And so, through prayer and meditation, we strive to deepen our connection with something greater than ourselves. Reasoning that it was our own inability to navigate life's issues led us to conclude that we might have a better opportunity at a fulfilling life if we could only find enough humility to understand the need for a better approach. The idea of a better path than the one we have tried and failed at is at the heart of this entire matter. Instead of having a mind open to other possibilities, we chose a path of our own construction to deliberately avoid and misrepresent life's challenges in an attempt to escape ownership of our own shortcomings or character defects.

Please don't take the easy way out of this by thinking somehow you are special and the entire universe conspired against you, so you are not responsible for the disaster addiction brought into your life. The hard, cold reality is that you are responsible for every bit of your reaction to the unfolding drama before you. Sure, other people or circumstances made things difficult, but ultimately, you chose a reaction to these issues that has proved to be detrimental to you and all those around you. The choice becomes clear and obvious that only you can decide to stay in that delusion or proceed toward something better.

Do you stop here at this juncture because you don't believe there is a higher power or that, if there is, you aren't willing to submit to whatever that belief might entail? This is what is often called a straw man argument. The point really isn't the higher power, the point is really your lack of humility. No one in the secular twelve-step rooms is going to exclude you from this process because you are agnostic or atheist. That really isn't the point. The truth is that sobriety must come first, no matter the religious, non-religious, spiritual, or mystical ideas you were either born into or migrated to. The idea of this book is to hopefully show you a path to sobriety that you can create for yourself.

It can be difficult to read the AA Big Book with its multiple references to God as well as its male-oriented view of the world, but those things are not the essence of the steps. The point is the realization that there is no miracle cure for addiction, and that being said, how do we get sober and also how do we maintain sobriety? It comes back to our own willingness to accept our responsibility. The very serious life and death-matter we deal with is only made easier with the fellowship we find in the twelve-step programs. Listening to others explain their past and their daily adventures in life gives us hope and the idea that we can also make it.

Chapter Ten

Step 12: The more you give, the more you get.

After making our way through the previous eleven steps, where do we go? The twelfth step explains this in its simple statement:

"Having had a spiritual awakening as the result of these steps, we tried to carry this message to alcoholics and to practice these principles in all our affairs."

First things first, maybe you didn't have a spiritual awakening. As discussed earlier, most of us have a gradual awakening that can take years to experience. Hopefully, you have progressed through the steps anyway. So here you are, a sober person looking forward to the future and wondering how to proceed. The real heart of this step is the focus on carrying the message forward and, most notably, practicing these principles in all our affairs.

As you would expect, after receiving a life philosophy that has changed your outlook and given you the tools to amend your life as needed, you are instructed to continue the process for the rest of your life. As you will hear in twelve-step rooms, you will never graduate from this course; you will be an eternal pilgrim on the quest for a serene life. Does that sound daunting? It shouldn't, as there is so much joy in a sober life. The key is never to forget the steps as life's challenges appear. Rest assured, you will face many opportunities to use the steps.

Another piece of this ongoing quest is the understanding that sharing your thoughts on sobriety and your story is valuable in maintaining your enthusiasm. One of the first revelations that came to Bill Wilson was the idea that in order to keep what he had gained in sobriety, he needed to give it away to others. This idea becomes a motivating factor for many in sobriety and, for some, a focal point of their sober life. The daily interactions with others help to keep us focused on the steps and how we apply them in daily life. One of the great gifts of this process is the comfort of knowing that advice and support are readily available from fellow pilgrims.

What would the Stoics say about step 12? Primarily they would emphasize the need to contribute to society through continued personal growth as well as mentoring others in their pursuit of a better life. As for the spiritual awakening, the Stoics might refer to that as the awareness that a better life is tied closely to developing your moral virtues and the quest to enhance them. Moral virtues aren't tied to any religion, philosophy, or institution but are a part of ourselves. We control this aspect of life and, for the most part, learn to appreciate the virtues as we go through life and learn from the outcomes of our thoughts and actions. This is the point in our journey when we become responsible for what we do and who we are becoming. The question now becomes, can we practice these principles in all our affairs? The answer I have found is not entirely, but the constant effort and careful consideration of outcomes move me forward on this pilgrimage to a better life.

A truly amazing revelation comes when during the process of discussing the steps with others, you gain an even deeper understanding. The benefit of becoming a sponsor of another pilgrim puts you in the role of an instructor and guide. Through this experience, you grow immensely. The real beauty of the process is the ability, through discussion with others, to come to a deeper understanding of life and our role in it.

As for Free Range Spirituality, step 12 is another example of the confluence of the step process and the desire for a better life through continued improvement. This last step reinforces the idea repeated in the rooms that the point is progress and not perfection. If you consider that spiritual life is a never-ending quest for serenity, courage, and fulfillment that comes through the progression of daily life, then you can find the essence of the 12 steps, Stoicism and Free-Range Spirituality.

Made in the USA
Middletown, DE
03 September 2024

60293529R00086